A Kid's Guide to BACKYARD ANIMALS

Eliza Berkowitz

illustrated by
Nicole LaRue

CONTENTS

MAMMALS

BIRDS

REPTILES

AMPHIBIANS

INVERTEBRATES

INTRODUCTION

Did you know that some backyard animals, like rabbits, can hop up to 45 miles per hour? Or that opossums can help control pests in your yard? You might already be familiar with squirrels, but have you ever seen a clever raccoon visiting your garbage cans at night? How about the fascinating skunk, which can spray you from 10 feet away? Whether you've spent years observing the wildlife in your backyard or are just beginning to learn, there's a world of wonder to explore!

This book will help you get familiar with the 40 backyard animals you're most likely to see in North America. Some of these animals are much more common than others. You'll learn about their habitats, diets, behaviors, and so much more. In a banner on the top of each page, you'll find the scientific name for each animal family—this is also known as the Latin name. And at the back of the book, there's a checklist to help you keep track of all the animals you have spotted. How many of the creatures in this book can you find?

Learning about backyard animals is fun for people of all ages. It's an activity the whole family can enjoy together. You don't need anything special to get started—just a curiosity for the many different critters that share our outdoor spaces.

TYPES OF ANIMALS

As you make your way through this book, you'll encounter many different kinds of animals.

Mammals are warm-blooded animals that have hair or fur on their bodies, breathe using lungs, produce milk to feed their young, and (almost always) give birth to live babies. Humans are mammals!

Birds are warm-blooded, feathered animals with wings and beaks or bills. Their young hatch from eggs and they communicate with each other by using songs or calls. A woodpecker is an example of a bird.

Reptiles are cold-blooded animals with scaly skin. They have lungs that help them breathe and they mostly reproduce by laying eggs (although some do give birth to live young). Snakes are reptiles.

Amphibians are cold-blooded with smooth, moist skin. They spend their early lives in water and later live on land. To be able to do this, they have both gills (for breathing underwater) and lungs (for breathing air). A salamander is a type of amphibian.

Invertebrates are animals that don't have a backbone. They are sometimes soft-bodied and other times have an exoskeleton, or a skeleton on the outside of their bodies that provides protection. They come in many different sizes and shapes. Worms are invertebrates. In fact, all insects are invertebrates!

DIY PROJECT

Have you ever been outside on a late spring evening and wondered what could be making so much noise? Maybe it sounded like croaking or high-pitched chirp sounds. If so, it could be that you were in the company of frogs. Maybe even many frogs. Different species make different sounds, but together their calls create a delightful soundscape. Invite frogs to your backyard by building a comfortable frog pond. To get started, gather the materials below:

ROCKS AND STONES OF DIFFERENT SHAPES AND SIZES

Next, find the perfect place to build your frog pond. You'll want to have enough room to place stones all around the outside of the container so frogs can easily hop up into the pond. You'll also want to add rocks inside to create a shallow area in the water for your new frog friends to rest. They will be most attracted to your pond if there's a mix of sun and shade, and also some plants. Watch as they discover their new backyard oasis.

WHAT'S IN MY BAG?

The next time you're looking for something to do, consider heading outside to try and spot some interesting wildlife. One thing it's important to remember is to observe wildlife from a distance. Many backyard animals are harmless, but it's best to be safe. You don't need any special supplies to become a backyard explorer, but here are a few things it might be helpful to have:

A **camera** is nice to have. When you've taken photos, you can go back and zoom in to get a better look. Or you may just want to save them as a nice reminder of the animals you've seen!

Wearing **sneakers** or **hiking boots** will keep your feet safe and comfortable if you're doing a lot of walking. When you're traveling in a wooded area, proper footwear can also prevent injuries.

A **hat** and **sunscreen** will help prevent sunburns.

Bug spray will keep the bugs away if you're in a wooded area or walking in tall grass.

Keep a **notebook** and **pen** handy. You never know when you might encounter an unusual animal and want to jot down its features or behaviors.

A **magnifying glass** can help you get a close-up look at smaller bugs. It will help you see details that you might have missed.

And finally, don't forget to bring **this book** to help you identify the animals you come across!

QUICK FACTS

Most common species: Little Brown Bat
Animal type: Mammal
Activity time: Nighttime (nocturnal)

BAT

Many people are scared of bats, thinking they're dangerous or threatening to humans. But bats are actually fascinating animals. They are the only mammals that can fly! With over 1,400 species, bats are found on every continent except Antarctica. They are social animals, often living in **colonies** that can range from just a few to thousands of bats.

Bats have wings that are formed by thin skin that stretches between their long fingers and extends down along their bodies. They have large ears and fur in shades of brown, gray, and black, often with patterns that help them **camouflage**.

food

SIZE

The little brown bat is medium-sized, with a 2- to 4-inch body length and a **wingspan** of 8 to 11 inches.

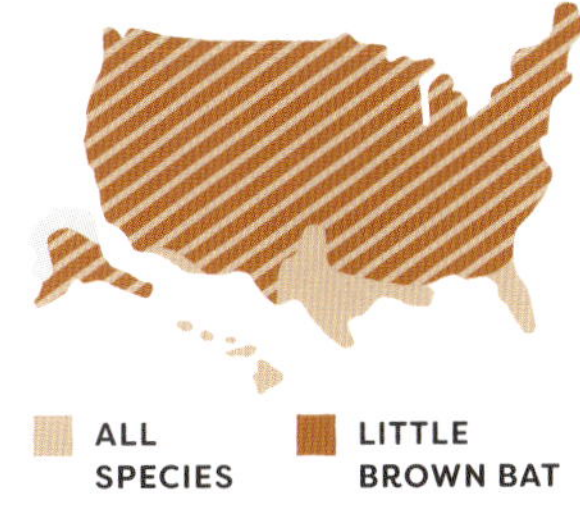

ALL SPECIES

LITTLE BROWN BAT

HABITAT & RANGE

Bats inhabit a wide range of environments, including forests, caves, deserts, and urban areas. They often roost in dark, sheltered places like caves, tree hollows, and buildings, where they can rest during the day and avoid **predators**. Bats are **adaptable** creatures and can thrive in various climates, from tropical rainforests to temperate regions and arid deserts.

WHAT IT EATS

Bats have different diets depending on the species. Most bat species, including the little brown bat, feed on insects, including moths, beetles, and mosquitoes. They play a crucial role in controlling pest populations.

FUN FACT

Some species of bats can fly up to 100 miles per hour!

QUICK FACTS

Most common species: American Black Bear
Animal type: Mammal
Activity time: Daytime (diurnal)

BEAR

In North America, the most common bears are the American black bear and the grizzly bear. It's natural to be scared of bears—they are quite large and have super-sharp claws and teeth. But bear attacks on humans are actually quite rare. If you do encounter a bear in the wild, stay calm. Facing the bear, talk in a calm voice as you slowly back away. If you're going to be in an area where you know there will be bears, it's best to carry bear spray.

Bears are sturdy and muscular. They're covered in thick fur, which helps them stay warm in cold climates. Their legs are short but powerful, making them great at digging and climbing. Their large paws have very sharp claws. Black bears can be different colors—many are black of course, but some are shades of brown, cinnamon, and blonde. Grizzly bears can be a range of different shades of brown.

SIZE

The American black bear weighs 90–500 pounds. The largest bear is the polar bear, found in the Arctic. Males can weigh up to 1,500 pounds—that's about as much as a grand piano!

tracks

ALL SPECIES

AMERICAN BLACK BEAR

HABITAT & RANGE

Black bears usually live in forested areas with lots of trees, shrubs, and plants. Grizzly bears live in the mountains. Polar bears live in the icy cold Arctic.

WHAT IT EATS

Bears prefer plants (especially berries and nuts!), but they also eat insects, meat, fish, and dead animals (also called **carrion**). Bears are definitely not picky eaters—they will happily eat human scraps or leftovers. It's important to never feed bears or leave food or garbage where they can easily get it.

claw detail

FUN FACT

Giant pandas are a type of bear that live in China and eat bamboo.

QUICK FACTS

Most common species: Bobcat (*Lynx rufus*)
Animal type: Mammal
Activity time: Daytime (diurnal)

BOBCAT

Lynx rufus

Bobcats are a type of wild cat that lives in North America. They get their name from their "bobbed" or short tails. They are excellent hunters and use their outstanding sight, hearing, and sense of smell to find **prey**. Their remarkable senses also help them avoid **predators**. Bobcats are **diurnal**, meaning they are active during the daytime.

Long-legged and with large paws, bobcats are easily identified by the tufts of hair on their ears. Their fur is light brown with darker spots and streaks all over except for their bellies, which are white.

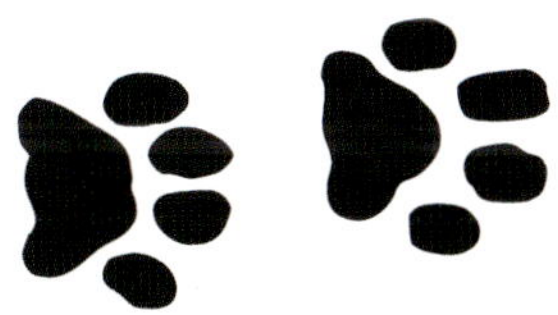

tracks

SIZE

Bobcats are medium sized—usually 28 to 40 inches long with a weight of 9 to 40 pounds.

BOBCAT

HABITAT & RANGE

Bobcats live in a range of **habitats** across North America. Forests, deserts, mountains, grasslands, and swamps are all home to bobcats. They especially like areas that are thick with plants that provide cover. Although they tend to avoid humans, bobcats are sometimes also found in suburban areas.

WHAT IT EATS

Eating mostly small to medium-sized animals, bobcats are **carnivores**. Their diet includes rabbits, rodents, birds, and sometimes larger animals like deer. When food isn't easily available, like in winter, they will **scavenge**, or eat whatever is around.

FUN FACT

Like other types of cats, bobcats are excellent hunters. They quietly stalk their prey and pounce at just the right time.

QUICK FACTS

Most common species: Eastern Chipmunk
Animal type: Mammal
Activity time: Daytime (diurnal)

CHIPMUNK

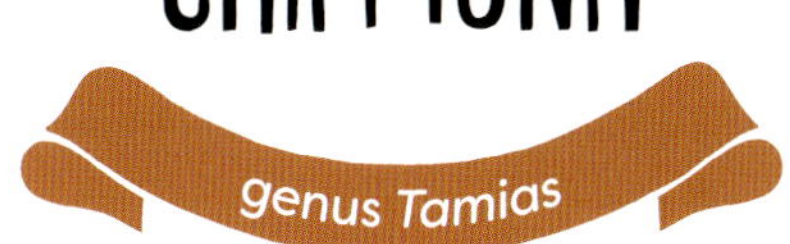

Chipmunks are small, energetic creatures known for their striped fur and adorable puffy cheeks. They belong to the squirrel family and are often seen scurrying around forests, parks, and gardens. There are 24 different species of chipmunk in North America. The chipmunks you are most likely to see are the Eastern chipmunk and the least chipmunk.

Chipmunks are easy to recognize by their small size, striped fur, and bushy tails. If you're lucky, you might catch one with its cheek pouches full of food that it's carrying back to its **burrow**, or underground home. Chipmunks also have sharp claws for digging and climbing, and strong teeth to gnaw on nuts and seeds.

SIZE

Chipmunks are 4 to 7 inches long, with their tails adding another 3 to 5 inches. They weigh between 1 and 5 ounces. The eastern chipmunk is a bit larger than other species—they can be 5 to 11 inches long.

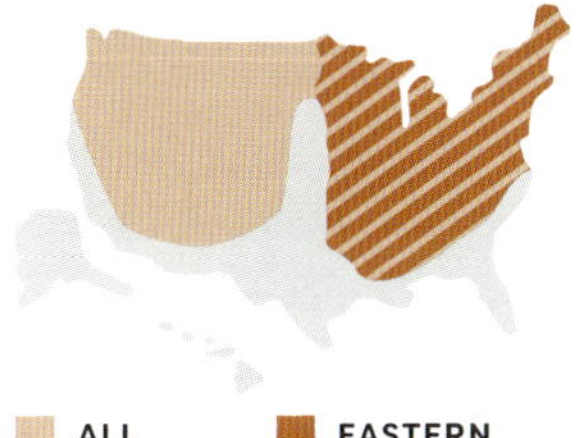

ALL SPECIES

EASTERN CHIPMUNK

HABITAT & RANGE

Chipmunks live in many **habitats**, like forests, gardens, and backyards. They prefer places where there are plenty of trees, shrubs, rocks, and places to hide, as well as lots of food sources. Chipmunks are ground-dwellers, meaning they spend most of their time on or near the ground, but they can also swim and climb trees.

WHAT IT EATS

Chipmunks are **omnivores**—they eat both plants and animals. They enjoy nuts, seeds, fruits, berries, insects, mushrooms, and plants. In the fall they prepare for winter by storing food in their underground **burrows**.

FUN FACT

A chipmunk's cheek pouches can grow to three times the size of its head to allow it to carry lots of food at once.

QUICK FACTS
Most common species: Coyote (*Canis latrans*)
Animal type: Mammal
Activity time: Nighttime (nocturnal)

COYOTE

Coyotes are members of the dog family. They look very similar to certain breeds of dog, like huskies and malamutes. Their differences mostly come down to the fact that coyotes are wild and dogs are **domesticated**. Coyotes aren't used to humans, so they would likely be shy or aggressive when encountering people. It's best to keep your distance if you see a coyote!

Coyotes are about the same size as medium-sized dogs. They are slim and athletic with long legs and a bushy tail. They are most often a grayish-brown color, but are sometimes tan or reddish in color.

SIZE

Coyotes usually weigh between 20 and 50 pounds. They grow to 3 to 4 feet long, including their tails, which are about a third of their length.

track

tooth

HABITAT & RANGE

Coyotes can thrive in many different environments. From deserts to forests to urban and suburban areas, coyotes live all over North America.

WHAT IT EATS

Coyotes are **omnivores**. They mostly eat small mammals like rodents and squirrels, but they also eat birds, insects, fruit, and grasses. They are definitely not choosy when it comes to food and will eat almost anything—in urban and suburban areas they will happily eat garbage or whatever scraps they can find.

FUN FACT

Coyotes communicate by using a bunch of different sounds. They howl, of course, but they also bark, growl, wail, yelp, huff, and squeal.

QUICK FACTS
Most common species: White-Tailed Deer
Animal type: Mammal
Activity time: Daytime (diurnal)

DEER

family Cervidae

Deer are graceful mammals known for their speed, agility, and beauty. Males, called **bucks**, grow antlers made of bone that shed and regrow each year. Female deer, called **does**, usually don't have antlers. Deer are very important to their **ecosystems**, as they help shape the forests and meadows where they live by eating certain plants. With large ears and sharp eyes, deer are excellent at sensing danger. They use their powerful legs to run quickly, escaping **predators** such as wolves and coyotes.

Deer are slender with short, smooth fur that is often reddish in the summer and grayish in the winter. Baby deer are usually born with white spots.

SIZE

Different species of deer grow to wildly different sizes. The white-tailed deer is 2.5 to 3 feet tall at the shoulder. The largest type of deer is the moose—they can grow to over 7 feet tall.

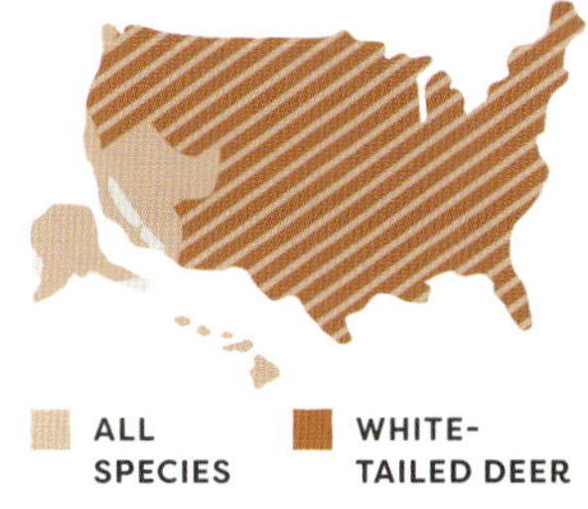

HABITAT & RANGE

Deer live in many different **habitats**, including forests, deserts, and swamps. They are one of very few animals that can survive on the **tundra**, with freezing temperatures and very little **vegetation**. Deer can be found on almost every continent, making them one of the most widespread animals in the world.

WHAT IT EATS

A deer's diet changes with the seasons. In spring and summer, they eat young, tender green plants, fruits, and berries. In fall, they'll also eat acorns and nuts. In winter, when there are few plants growing, they will eat the tough woody stems of plants, bushes, and trees.

FUN FACT

There are about 30 different species of deer around the world, including Santa's favorite, the reindeer!

QUICK FACTS
Most common species: American Elk
Animal type: Mammal
Activity time: Daytime (diurnal)

Elk are members of the deer family. In North America, elk are commonly found in the Rocky Mountains, the Pacific Northwest, and parts of the eastern United States. They are social animals and live in herds, especially in the winter. Male elk are called bulls and they have antlers that can grow to 4 feet and weigh up to 40 pounds. Their antlers fall out and regrow each year.

The first thing you might notice if you encounter an elk is its impressive size. They are muscular with long legs and a thick neck. Males often have a mane of long hair. The elk's fur color changes with the seasons. They are usually dark brown or tan in summer, with lighter cream-colored patches. In winter, their fur becomes thicker and darker, helping to keep them warm in the cold weather.

SIZE

Elk are one of the largest species of deer. Their size varies quite a lot depending on the region. The largest male elk can grow to 1,100 pounds!

HABITAT & RANGE

Elk are found in a range of **habitats**, including forests, grasslands, and in the mountains. They prefer open areas with access to food and cover for protection from **predators**. They **migrate**, or move from one area to another, when the seasons change.

WHAT IT EATS

Elk enjoy a diet of grasses, shrubs, leaves, and bark. They especially like the tender plants in the spring and summer. In the winter, they mostly eat twigs and bark from trees and shrubs. They have special stomachs that allow them to digest tough plant matter.

FUN FACT

Elk have two teeth called "ivories" that are made of the same stuff as tusks on walruses and elephants.

QUICK FACTS

Most common species: Red Fox
Animal type: Mammal
Activity time: Nighttime (nocturnal)

FOX

Foxes are super smart, athletic mammals that live all over the world. Foxes are so common that they show up in the folklore of many different cultures. Because they are so smart, they are usually depicted as being clever and tricky. Red foxes, named for the color of their coats, are the most common type of fox in North America.

Slim and graceful, foxes are often mistaken for coyotes or wolves. Their fur can be reddish-brown, gray, white, or black depending on the species. They have pointed snouts, short legs, and large perky ears. Their long, bushy tails help them to balance and also to communicate with other foxes.

SIZE

Foxes usually weigh 6 to 17 pounds and are 32 to 57 inches long. Their long tails make up about a third of their length. Male foxes are a bit larger than the females.

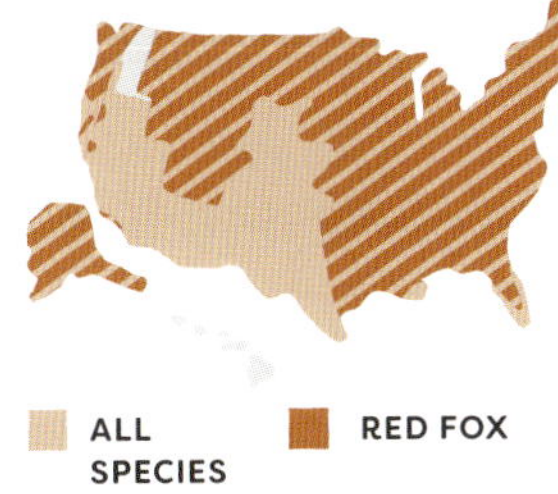

HABITAT & RANGE

Foxes can **adapt** to many different environments. They are found in forests, mountains, deserts, grasslands, and suburban and urban areas.

WHAT IT EATS

Foxes are **omnivores**. They are excellent hunters, so the bulk of their diet is small mammals, like birds, rodents, and rabbits. They also eat fruit, insects, and even reptiles. In urban areas, foxes are known to comb through garbage looking for something to eat.

FUN FACT

Foxes have a distinct, smelly odor. That's right—they stink! At the base of their tails, they have glands that release a terrible scent.

QUICK FACTS

Most common species: House Mouse
Animal type: Mammal
Activity time: Nighttime (nocturnal)

MOUSE

Mice are small, furry rodents known for their curious and active nature and ability to reproduce in large numbers. They are social animals, often living together in groups. They are most active at night and although they don't have great vision, they do have excellent senses of smell and hearing. The most common mouse in North America is the house mouse, named because it will go into houses looking for food.

Mice are little, with pointed snouts and large ears compared to their heads. Their fur is usually short and can vary in color, including shades of gray, brown, or white. Mice have long, hairless tails that help with balance and communication, and their whiskers are highly sensitive, helping them get around in the dark.

SIZE

Mice are generally small, with body lengths ranging from 2.5 to 4 inches, not including the tail, which is usually about the same length as their body. Their weight typically falls between 0.5 to 1 ounce.

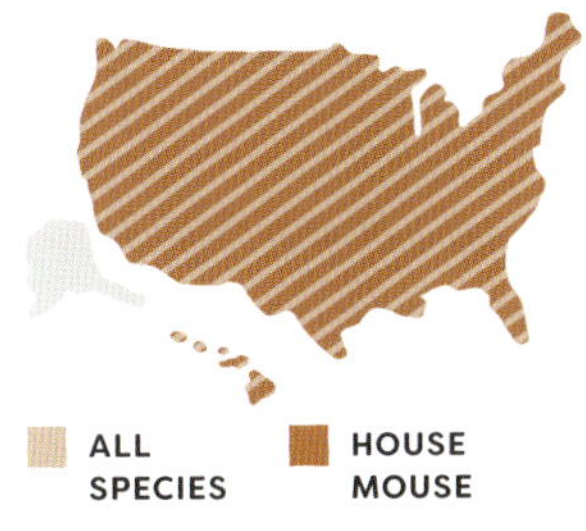

HABITAT & RANGE

Mice can thrive in many different **habitats**, including forests, grasslands, fields, and urban areas. They often build their nests in places like **burrows**, under logs, or in buildings where they can find food and safety. The house mouse does well in human environments and can be found in homes, farms, and warehouses.

WHAT IT EATS

Mice are **omnivorous** and eat many different things. They primarily feed on grains, seeds, fruits, and vegetables, but they will also eat small insects, nuts, and even scraps of human food.

FUN FACT

Many people consider mice to be pests. But other people keep them as pets! A fancy mouse is a mouse that has been bred to live as a pet. These are the kind of mice they sell in pet stores.

QUICK FACTS

Most common species: Virginia Opossum
Animal type: Mammal
Activity time: Nighttime (nocturnal)

OPOSSUM

Opossums, also called possums, might look like rodents, but they're actually **marsupials**. They're related to the kangaroo and the koala. Like other marsupials, after a female gives birth she keeps her babies warm and safe in her pouch. When the babies are ready to live outside the pouch, the mom carries her babies around on her back. The Virginia opossum is the only species of opossum **native** to North America, but different species live in other places, like Central and South America.

An opossum has a pointy face, pink nose, dark eyes, and long whiskers. Its fur is white and gray and it has a long, hairless tail.

SIZE

Their long tails take up about half their total length, which can be up to 40 inches. The Virginia opossum is about the size of a house cat.

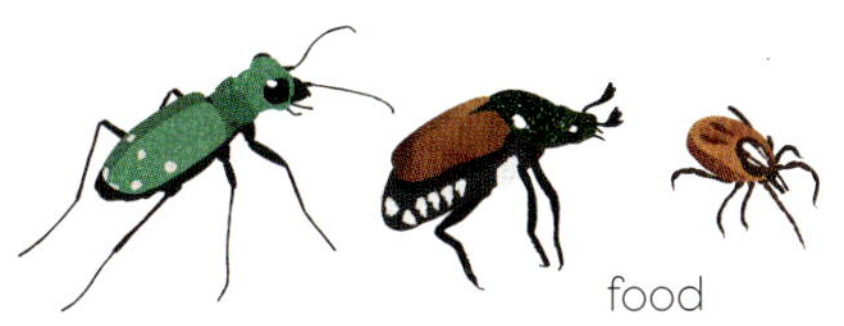

food

ALL SPECIES
VIRGINIA OPOSSUM

HABITAT & RANGE

Able to **adapt** to many **habitats**, opossums can live in forests, wetlands, farmland, and urban and suburban areas.

WHAT IT EATS

Opossums are **omnivores**—they eat everything! Their favorite foods are insects, small mammals, fruits, vegetables, eggs, and **carrion**. They play an important role in their environment by eating unwanted pests, like ticks and beetles.

FUN FACT

When opossums feel scared, they drop to the ground and play dead. They can stay this way for several hours!

QUICK FACTS
Most common species: Black-Tailed Prairie Dog
Animal type: Mammal
Activity time: Daytime (diurnal)

PRAIRIE DOG

Prairie dogs are small rodents known for their social behavior and their well-constructed underground homes. Despite their name, they are actually a type of ground squirrel. They get their name from the sound of their calls, which sound like a dog barking.

Prairie dogs have short, muscular bodies covered in thick light brown fur that keeps them warm in the winter. They have short, furry tails that are 3 to 4 inches long. They have sharp claws that they use like tiny shovels to dig deep into the ground. They also have large, round eyes that sit high on their heads, giving them a good view of their surroundings to keep an eye out for **predators**.

SIZE

Prairie dogs are small to medium-sized. They measure 12 to 16 inches long, including their tails. They usually weigh 1 to 3 pounds.

HABITAT & RANGE

Prairie dogs live in the open grasslands and prairies of North America. They are most common in the central and western United States, as well as parts of Mexico and Canada. Their underground homes are carefully constructed to keep them cool in the summer and warm in the winter. Their **burrows** also provide safety from predators and bad weather.

WHAT IT EATS

Prairie dogs are **herbivores**, so they mostly eat plants, like grasses, seeds, roots, flowers, and vegetables. They may also eat insects on occasion.

FUN FACT

Prairie dogs are burrowing experts. Their burrows are like tiny cities, with complex tunnels and rooms. They even have separate areas for sleeping, keeping food, raising babies, and going to the bathroom!

QUICK FACTS
Most common species: Eastern Cottontail
Animal type: Mammal
Activity time: Daytime (diurnal)

RABBIT

Rabbits are adorable, furry animals known for their long ears, twitchy noses, and impressive hopping abilities. They are gentle creatures that live in many places around the world—maybe even in your own backyard! Wild rabbits roam freely outside, unlike **domesticated** rabbits that people keep as pets. There are 28 different species of rabbit, but the eastern cottontail is the most common in North America. Some species of rabbits can hop 35 to 45 miles an hour!

Rabbits have silky fur, large ears, and cotton-puff tails. Some have solid-color fur in shades of brown, gray, white, or black and others have patterned fur. They have long ears that help them hear well and strong back legs to jump high and run fast to escape from **predators**.

SIZE

The eastern cottontail is 15 to 18 inches long and weighs 1.8 to 3 pounds. Pet rabbits can be larger or smaller—some breeds, like the Flemish Giant, can grow to 20 pounds and measure over 30 inches long!

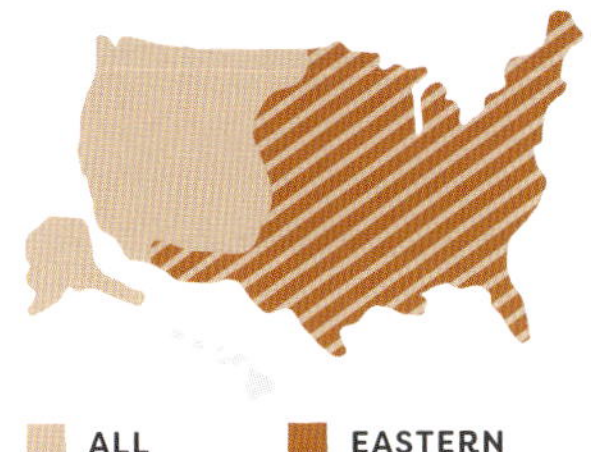

HABITAT & RANGE

Rabbits live in a variety of **habitats**, including grasslands, forests, farms, and urban areas. Some even live in desert areas, where their long ears help them keep cool by releasing heat.

WHAT IT EATS

Rabbits are **herbivores**, or plant-eaters. Their favorite foods include grasses, fruits, vegetables, herbs, and flowers. Rabbits need to munch on food constantly to keep their teeth—which never stop growing—worn down.

tail

FUN FACT

Baby rabbits are called kittens.

QUICK FACTS

Most common species: North American Raccoon
Animal type: Mammal
Activity time: Nighttime (nocturnal)

RACCOON

Raccoons are known for being smart, playful, sneaky, and curious. You may not see these critters much, because they're **nocturnal**—they sleep during the day and are active at night. They're happy to dig through garbage bins, using their little paws like hands to grab food. Raccoons are also excellent climbers. Their sharp claws help them climb trees, fences, and buildings to hang out in high places during the day.

Raccoons have black fur around their eyes that makes them look like they're wearing a bandit mask. This isn't just for show—it helps them see better at night by reducing glare from lights. They use their long, fluffy tails with rings of black and gray fur to help keep warm. Their tails also help them balance when they climb trees.

tracks

SIZE

Raccoons usually weigh 22 pounds or less, but some adult males can grow to 44 pounds.

ALL SPECIES

NORTH AMERICAN RACCOON

HABITAT & RANGE

They live in many different **habitats**, such as forests, urban areas, and agricultural areas. Some species prefer colder weather, while others can survive in tropical areas.

WHAT IT EATS

Raccoons are not picky when it comes to food—they like fruit, insects, nuts, fish, and even leftovers from humans. They'll eat almost anything they can find, making them really good at surviving in different places.

FUN FACT

One of the funniest things about raccoons is that they sometimes dunk their food in water before eating it. Scientists aren't sure why they do this, but it looks like they're giving their meal a good wash!

QUICK FACTS
Most common species: Common Striped Skunk
Animal type: Mammal
Activity time: Nighttime (nocturnal)

SKUNK

Skunks are best known for their black-and-white fur and for the smelly spray they give off when they are threatened. The smell is so bad that it sends **predators** running in the other direction. Skunks only spray when they are defending themselves. If you come across a skunk and it starts stomping its feet, it's giving you a clear warning that it may spray. In North America, the common striped skunk is the species you're most likely to see.

Different skunk species have different markings, but the common striped skunk is black with a white v-shape down its back. It also has a white bar-shaped spot between its eyes. The spotted skunk has white stripes patterned all down its body. It also has a thick, fluffy tail.

SIZE

About the size of a pet cat, the common striped skunk will grow to 18 to 32 inches long. They weigh up to 13 pounds.

HABITAT & RANGE

Skunks are able to survive in many environments. They are found in forests, farmlands, grasslands, and even urban and suburban areas.

WHAT IT EATS

A skunk's diet changes with the seasons. An **omnivore**, it eats both plant and animal matter, including insects, small mammals, birds, eggs, fruits, vegetables, and grubs. They especially love to eat insects that live in the ground, like beetles and grasshoppers.

tracks

FUN FACT

A skunk's spray can be smelled a mile away.

QUICK FACTS

Most common species: Eastern Gray Squirrel
Animal type: Mammal
Activity time: Daytime (diurnal)

SQUIRREL

Squirrels are energetic, bushy-tailed animals that are commonly seen scurrying up trees in parks. They're fun to watch because they're always very busy climbing, jumping, and searching for food. If you have trees in your backyard, it's a safe bet that you'll spot some squirrels if you keep a lookout for them.

Squirrels have fluffy tails that help them balance as they jump from tree to tree. They also use their tail like a blanket, wrapping it around themselves to keep warm in cold weather. Squirrels are excellent climbers due to their sharp claws and strong back legs. Their fur color varies depending on the species—some are gray, red, or brown, and others might even be black or white.

SIZE

Most squirrels are pretty small. They usually weigh between just 1 and 2 pounds. They're 10 to 20 inches long, including their tails, which make up about half of that length.

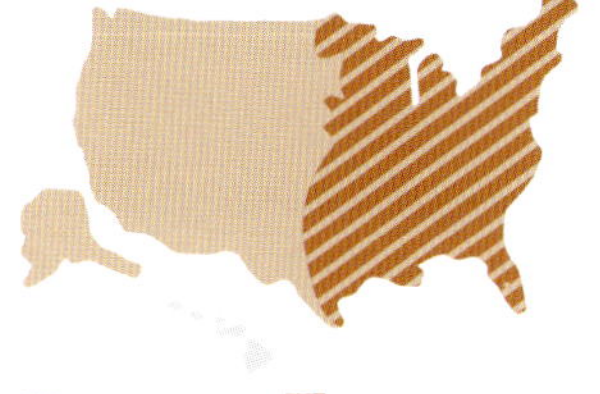

ALL SPECIES

EASTERN GRAY SQUIRREL

HABITAT & RANGE

Squirrels are most often found in forests, parks, and backyards where there are plenty of trees to climb and food to find. They make their homes out of leaves and twigs, building them high up in tree branches. Some squirrels, like ground squirrels, live in **burrows** dug into the ground.

WHAT IT EATS

Squirrels are **omnivores**, which means they eat both plants and animals, though their favorite foods are plant-based: nuts, seeds, fruits, and vegetables. They also eat insects, small animals, and eggs.

FUN FACT

Squirrels are very smart and have excellent memories, which helps them remember where they've buried their food.

QUICK FACTS

Most common species: Meadow Vole
Animal type: Mammal
Activity time: Daytime (diurnal)

VOLE

genus Microtus

Voles are small rodents that are often mistaken for mice or rats due to their size and shape. They spend most of their time in underground **burrows** that they dig or in **vegetation** above ground. Voles are very social and can often be found in groups. The most common type of vole in North America is called the meadow vole.

Voles have compact, strong bodies with a short, rounded snout and a short tail. Their fur is usually thick and soft, in colors that range from brown to gray or reddish-brown. Voles have small eyes and ears, which are often somewhat hidden by their fur. Their limbs are short, which helps them dig in the dirt.

SIZE

Voles can range in size from 4 to 10 inches in length, including the tail. They usually weigh between 2 and 9 ounces, depending on the species. The meadow vole is about 6 inches long and weighs about 1.5 ounces—the same as a slice of bread!

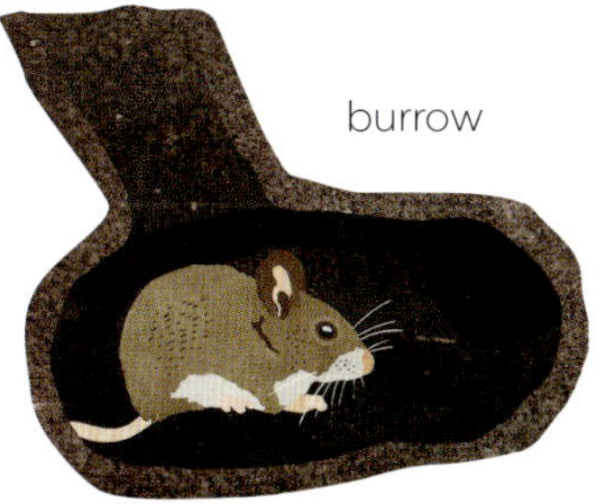

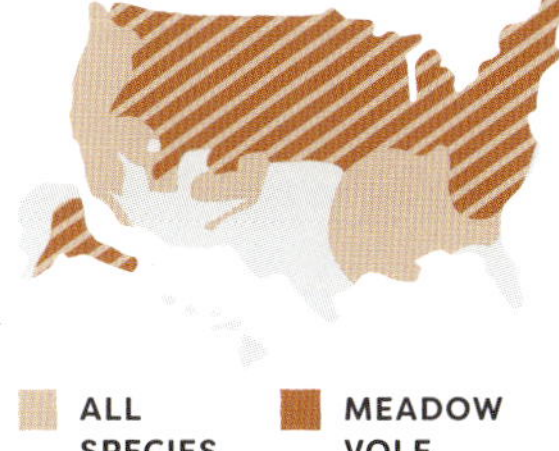

HABITAT & RANGE

Voles live in a variety of environments, depending on the species. They live in grasslands, forests, and wetlands. They can be found in North America, Europe, and Asia.

WHAT IT EATS

Voles are **herbivores**. They mostly feed on grasses, seeds, roots, and other plant material. They may also eat bark and tubers in winter when there isn't much green vegetation to be found.

FUN FACT

Voles can cause major damage in lawns and gardens as they tunnel through the land, scarfing up roots and plants.

QUICK FACTS

Most common species: Northern Cardinal
Animal type: Bird
Activity time: Daytime (diurnal)

CARDINAL

When you spot a bright red northern cardinal, you can be sure it's a male. Their faces are black, their beaks are red, and they have long tails. The female is more of a grayish color, with some red in its wing feathers and a red-tipped crest.

Cardinals are known for their sweet singing. They are also known to be tough. The males will attack any bird that threatens its territory.

Most cardinals choose their mates for life, and share the duties of feeding and raising their young.

SIZE

The average cardinal is 8.3 to 9.1 inches in length with a **wingspan** of 9.8 to 12.2 inches.

HABITAT & RANGE

Cardinals live in a variety of **habitats**. They look for areas that are thick with shrubs and foliage. They used to only be found in warmer climates, but are now spotted all over the eastern United States and up into parts of Canada.

WHAT IT EATS

Northern cardinals eat fruits, including wild grapes and blackberries. They also eat seeds (sunflower seeds are their favorite) and many kinds of insects, including centipedes and katydids.

FUN FACT

When a male cardinal is interested in a female cardinal, it will find seeds and feed them to her.

QUICK FACTS
Most common species: Mallard
Animal type: Bird
Activity time: Daytime (diurnal)

DUCK

Ducks belong to the same family as swans and geese, so it's no surprise they like to spend time in the water. On land their walk is best described as a waddle. Often seen together in groups, ducks are social animals and move in flocks. There are about 100 species of ducks that live all over the world. The mallard, with its shimmering green head and orange legs, is the most common kind of duck in North America.

Ducks can be many different colors depending on the species. Male ducks are usually more colorful, with bright shades of blue, green, and patterns. Female ducks have more muted colors. Ducks have wide, flat beaks that help them get food from below the water's surface and their webbed feet make them great swimmers.

SIZE

Varying in size, most ducks are between 15 and 30 inches long with a weight of 1 to 3 pounds.

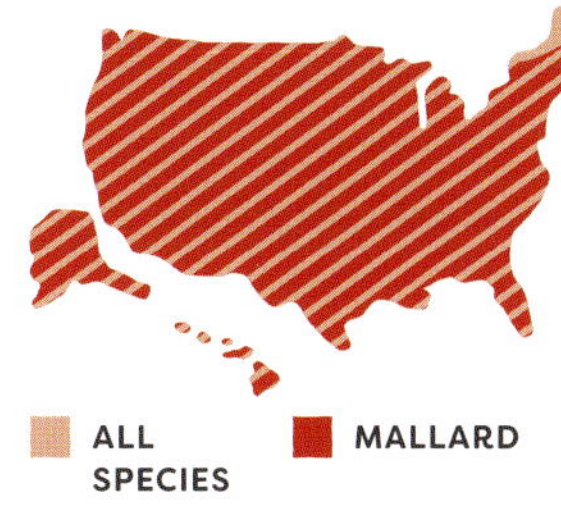

ALL SPECIES
MALLARD

HABITAT & RANGE

Ducks are found in a wide range of wetland **habitats**, near lakes, ponds, rivers, marshes, coastal areas, and grasslands.

WHAT IT EATS

Ducks are **omnivores** and eat a variety of foods. They enjoy different types of plants, seeds, insects, small fish, and grains.

FUN FACT

Not all ducks quack! The classic quacking sound that we think of when we think of ducks is the call of the female mallard.

egg

QUICK FACTS

Most common species: Canada Goose
Animal type: Bird
Activity time: Daytime (diurnal)

GOOSE

Canada geese are easily identified by their distinctive black heads and necks. They are social animals, often seen in pairs or flocks, traveling in V-shaped formations in the sky. Their distinctive honking calls are used to communicate with each other.

Canada geese have mostly brown bodies with a black head and neck. They have white patches on their cheeks and under their necks. Their wings are long and powerful, allowing them to fly long distances. They have webbed feet which allow them to swim easily through water.

food

SIZE

Canada geese vary in size. They usually are between 30 and 43 inches long with a **wingspan** of up to 6 feet. Adults usually weigh between 5.5 and 14.5 pounds.

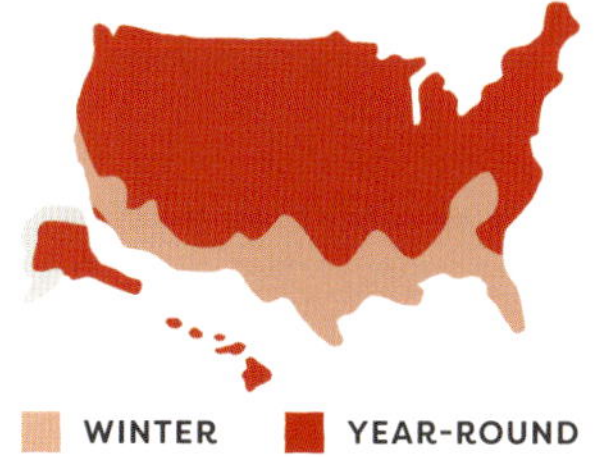

HABITAT & RANGE

Canada geese live in areas where they can find both water and open grassy fields. They're found all over North America. Canada geese often live near lakes, ponds, rivers, and marshes. They enjoy grazing in open fields and parks, and have even been found living in urban areas.

WHAT IT EATS

In warmer months, Canada geese eat mostly grass. In cooler months, they rely on berries and seeds. They are known to be fond of blueberries and corn.

FUN FACT

A flock of geese is called a gaggle.

QUICK FACTS
Most common species: Red-Tailed Hawk
Animal type: Bird
Activity time: Daytime (diurnal)

HAWK

Hawks are typically medium to large in size, found in a variety of **habitats** across the world. Known for their sharp vision and predatory nature, these **carnivores** can spot their next meal from far away. You can sometimes catch hawks soaring in circles in the sky.

Hawks are usually brown, black, white, or gray in color, with hooked beaks, large eyes, and yellow talons. The red-tailed hawk, the most common type of hawk in North America, has broad wings and a tail with reddish orange feathers.

SIZE

The size of a hawk depends on the species. Small species, like the sharp-shinned hawk, are 9 to 14 inches long. The red-tailed hawk is a medium- to large-size bird with an average length of 18 to 26 inches. The ferruginous hawk is the largest hawk in North America. Its length is 20 to 27 inches.

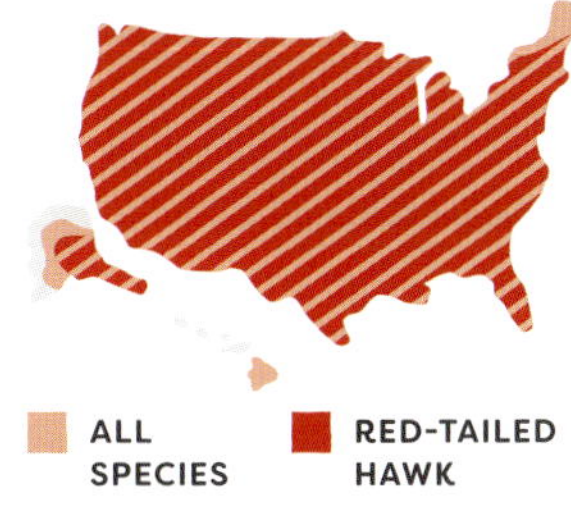

ALL SPECIES

RED-TAILED HAWK

HABITAT & RANGE

Hawks live in open habitats throughout the United States and most of Canada. They live in many types of environments, as long as they have high places to perch and some open land for hunting.

WHAT IT EATS

Hawks mostly eat small- to medium-sized animals. They often prey on rodents such as mice, voles, and rabbits. They also eat smaller birds, reptiles, and insects.

FUN FACT

Hawks are fast flyers. They can reach speeds of 120 miles per hour when diving.

egg

QUICK FACTS

Most common species: Ruby-Throated Hummingbird
Animal type: Bird
Activity time: Daytime (diurnal)

HUMMINGBIRD

Hummingbirds may be the world's smallest bird, but they have huge personalities. Often seen as a symbol of joy and resilience, it's exciting to be in the presence of these high-energy birds. You can encourage them to visit your yard by planting **native** flowering plants and maintaining a hummingbird feeder. The most common type of hummingbird in North America is the ruby-throated hummingbird. It is easy to identify by the red color on its throat.

Hummingbirds have colorful feathers, which can shimmer in shades of green, blue, red, and purple. Males are usually more colorful than females, using their brilliant feathers to attract mates. They use their long, slender beaks to reach nectar inside flowers. Their wings beat so fast that they create the humming sound these birds are named for.

SIZE

Hummingbirds are usually 2 to 5 inches long. The ruby-throated hummingbird is about 3.75 inches long and weighs 0.1 to 0.2 ounces, as light as one or two pennies!

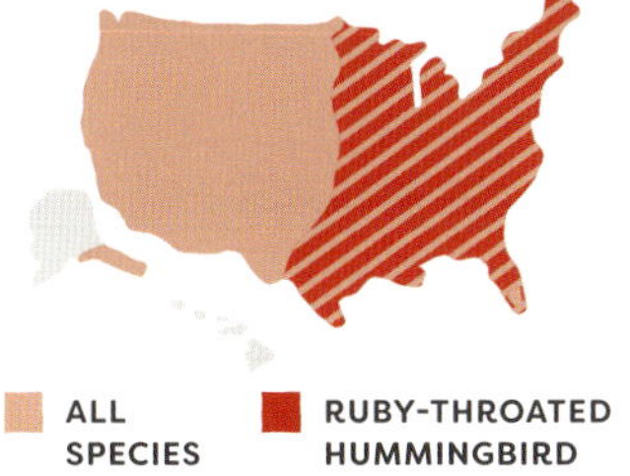

HABITAT & RANGE

Hummingbirds live in diverse **habitats** across North and South America, from forests and gardens to deserts and mountain slopes.

WHAT IT EATS

Hummingbirds primarily feed on nectar from flowers, which provides the fuel they need to keep up their busy lives. To get protein, they also eat small insects and spiders.

FUN FACT

Most hummingbird feeders are red because hummingbirds are naturally drawn to that color. In nature, red flowers tend to be a good source of food.

egg

QUICK FACTS

Most common species: Great Horned Owl
Animal type: Bird
Activity time: Nighttime (nocturnal)

OWL

If you're hoping to spot an owl, you will need to have a great deal of patience. During the day owls can be found perched high up in tree branches. At night they prefer open areas for hunting. The best way to know if there's an owl nearby is to listen for their hooting, screeching, or whistling sounds. There are about 250 different species of owls around the world—the great horned owl being the most common in North America.

Owls **camouflage**, or blend into their environment. The patterns and colors of their feathers can match the landscape, whether that be the brown bark of a tree or the Arctic's white snow. They usually have big, round eyes, flat faces, and hooked beaks. They also have large feet with super-sharp talons.

SIZE

Depending on the species, owls can be anywhere from 5 to 28 inches in length, with **wingspans** that reach from 1 foot to 6.6 feet. Great horned owls are 19 to 35 inches tall, with a wingspan of about 4.6 feet.

ALL SPECIES

GREAT HORNED OWL

HABITAT & RANGE

Owls can be found in almost every **habitat**. They live on every continent except for Antarctica.

WHAT IT EATS

Owls are **carnivores**, or meat eaters. Large owls consume rodents and small birds. Smaller owls mostly eat insects. They use their amazing hearing to help with hunting—they can pinpoint the slightest sounds with accuracy!

FUN FACT

Owls swallow their **prey** whole. Later, they cough up small pellets of bones, fur, feathers, and other bits that didn't get digested.

egg

QUICK FACTS

Most common species: Rock Pigeon
Animal type: Bird
Activity time: Daytime (diurnal)

PIGEON

Often seen in a flock with other pigeons, these medium-sized birds spend much of their time looking for food. They walk or run while pecking at the ground, picking up seeds as they go. Rock pigeons are known to fly away when startled—keep still if you want to watch them!

You can recognize a rock pigeon by its plump body, short legs, iridescent feathers on the throat, and orange-colored eyes.

SIZE

Rock pigeons range from 11.8 to 14.2 inches in length, with a **wingspan** of 19.7 to 26.4 inches.

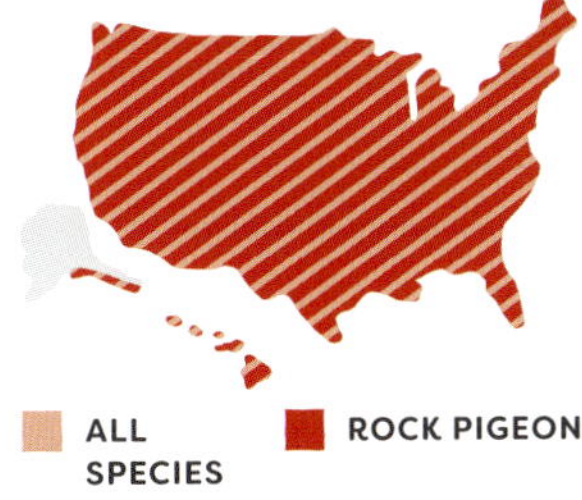

HABITAT & RANGE

Pigeons mostly live in towns and urban areas. You can often see large flocks at city parks, where they peck at scraps from humans.

WHAT IT EATS

They are not picky eaters. In the wild, they eat seeds and fruit. In parks, people often feed them breadcrumbs, and they will also peck at any food garbage left behind.

FUN FACT

Male and female pigeons work together to make a nest. The male picks the spot and finds materials, like straw, stems, and sticks, for the female. She then uses those materials to build the nest.

QUICK FACTS

Most common species: American Robin
Animal type: Bird
Activity time: Daytime (diurnal)

ROBIN

It's true what they say, the early bird does get the worm! In the early mornings, American robins can be found waiting patiently on lawns for a worm to pop up. They begin their musical chirping about an hour before the sun rises and also sing at dusk to attract a mate and mark their territory.

Adult male robins have gray-brown feathers with orange or red on their chest. Females and young males are duller in color. All robins have large, round bodies, yellow beaks, long legs, and tails with white tips at the corners.

SIZE

The American robin is 8 to 11 inches long with a **wingspan** between 12.2 and 15.8 inches.

egg

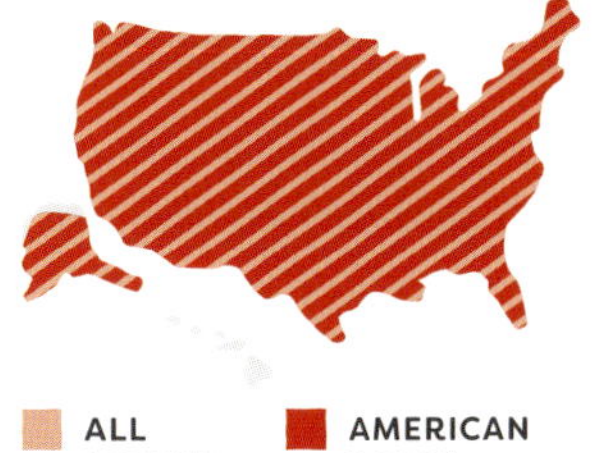

ALL SPECIES

AMERICAN ROBIN

HABITAT & RANGE

American robins are common all over North America. You can find them in backyards, parks, and fields. They are also found in more wild areas, like forests and woodlands.

WHAT IT EATS

The American robin's favorite food is earthworms. In the early mornings, they hang out on lawns, waiting for a wriggly worm to appear. When they spot one, they quickly snatch it! They also enjoy berries and fruit, which they usually eat later in the day, though it's their primary food in the winter.

FUN FACT

Robins can live up to 13 years, but in the wild they usually live only one to two years.

QUICK FACTS

Most common species: Downy Woodpecker
Animal type: Bird
Activity time: Daytime (diurnal)

WOODPECKER

Woodpeckers are a type of bird known for the hammering sounds they make. They spend most of their lives in trees and use their strong beaks to drill holes into wood. They do this for a few reasons. Sometimes they are looking for insects to eat. Other times they are creating nests or storing food.

Woodpeckers often have brightly colored and patterned feathers. Their strong beaks are shaped like chisels, helping them make holes in trees. They have a stiff, pointed tail that helps them balance while climbing and their feet have special toes that hold tight to tree trunks and branches.

SIZE

There are many species of woodpeckers and their sizes vary. The downy woodpecker is an example of a small woodpecker—it is only about 6 inches long. Larger species, like the pileated woodpecker, can grow over 18 inches in length.

egg

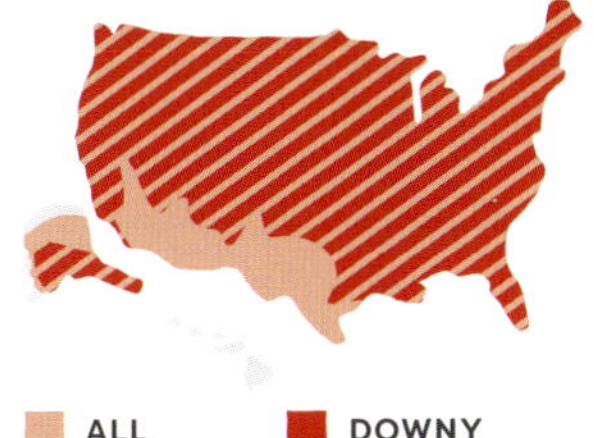

HABITAT & RANGE

Woodpeckers live all over the world except in Australia, New Guinea, Madagascar, and New Zealand, as well as the polar regions. You can find them living in a wide range of environments, including forests, woodlands, and urban areas.

WHAT IT EATS

Most woodpeckers eat insects. They do this by drilling holes into tree trunks and using their long tongues to grab beetles, ants, and other bugs. Some species, like the red-bellied woodpecker, also consume fruits, nuts, and seeds. Another type of woodpecker, the sapsucker, is known to lap up nutrient-rich sap from holes they've drilled.

FUN FACT

Woodpeckers' feet have two toes facing forward and two toes facing backward. This helps them get a good grip on trees.

QUICK FACTS
Most common species: Five-Lined Skink
Animal type: Reptile
Activity time: Daytime (diurnal)

LIZARD

Lizards are reptiles. There are many types of lizards—over 3,000 species in fact! They are known for their speed and climbing skills, both of which come in handy when hunting for food and escaping **predators**. They have excellent eyesight and some lizards are even able to see in color.

Lizards have dry, scaly skin that protects them in different environments. Most lizards have four legs, with five sharp claws on each foot. They have long tails, which are sometimes used for balance or for storing fat. Many lizards, like the chameleon, can change the color of their skin to **camouflage**, or blend in with their surroundings.

SIZE

Lizards come in many sizes. Some, like the dwarf gecko, are tiny—under 2 inches long. Others, like the Komodo dragon, are huge—they can grow up to 10 feet long! The five-lined skink is 5 to 8.5 inches long, including its tail.

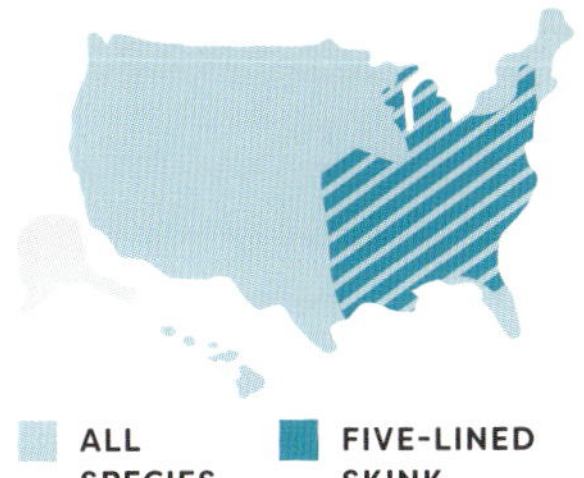

HABITAT & RANGE

Lizards are found all over the world, on every continent except Antarctica. They can live in many different **habitats**. They are commonly found in deserts, rainforests, jungles, grasslands, and even in urban areas.

WHAT IT EATS

Lizards have a wide variety of diets depending on the species. Most lizards eat insects, such as flies, crickets, and spiders. Others eat only plants, like leaves, fruit, and flowers. Many larger lizards eat other animals, including birds, small mammals, and even other reptiles.

FUN FACT

Many lizards can drop their tails if they're caught by a predator. The tail will keep wiggling to distract the predator, so the lizard can make its escape.

QUICK FACTS

Most common species: Common Garter Snake
Animal type: Reptile
Activity time: Daytime (diurnal)

SNAKE

Snakes are really cool animals that get around by slithering on the ground. Since they can't walk (they don't have legs!), they use their strong muscles to move smoothly over grass, rocks, and even up trees. Some snakes, like cobras or rattlesnakes, are **venomous**, but most snakes are harmless to humans and are actually quite shy. There are more than 3,400 snake species. The most frequently seen snake in North America is the common garter snake. They are small and come in different colors. Their venom is mild and unlikely to cause serious harm.

Snakes have long, thin, cylindrical bodies without arms and legs. They are able to move their muscles and scales quietly, hardly making a sound. They come in many colors and often **camouflage** with their surroundings.

SIZE

Snakes vary greatly in size. The common garter snake (including its tail) is about 22 inches long—but the largest ones can grow to about 54 inches!

open jaw

HABITAT & RANGE

In tropical areas you'll find the greatest number of snake species, but snakes thrive in a wide range of **habitats**. They can live in deserts and rainforests, and even in lakes and oceans! In North America, Alaska is the only place where there are no **native** snakes.

WHAT IT EATS

Snakes eat a wide variety of foods depending on their size, including insects, amphibians, rodents, birds, eggs, other snakes, or even larger animals. Snakes don't chew their food. Instead, they swallow it whole. Their jaws open wide enough to swallow small animals in one big gulp!

FUN FACT

Snakes use their tongues to smell. They stick out their tongues to "sniff" the air. They do this to find food or sense danger.

QUICK FACTS
Most common species: Painted Turtle
Animal type: Reptile
Activity time: Daytime (diurnal)

TURTLE

Turtles are reptiles best known for their hard, patterned shells and for being slow on land. There are many types of turtles, about 350 species in all. Painted turtles are the most common type in North America. Some types of turtles make great pets and others can be dangerous. Never handle a turtle in the wild unless you know it is safe—snapping turtles, for example, can have a nasty bite.

Turtles are covered in a hard shell that can vary in size, color, and shape. Their heads are bony and they have beak-like mouths. Some turtles can pull their heads back into their shells for protection, but others cannot.

SIZE

Turtles vary significantly in size. The smallest turtles can be as small as 3 or 4 inches long, while the largest can be over 6 feet long. The leatherback sea turtle can weigh 2,000 pounds! Painted turtles are usually 5 to 9 inches long, and the female is larger than the male.

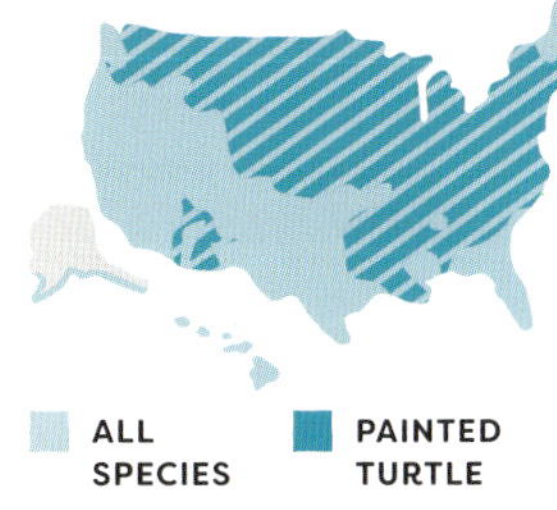

HABITAT & RANGE

Turtles can live both on land and in the water. Freshwater turtles are often found in ponds, lakes, rivers, and wetlands, while marine turtles inhabit oceans and coastal areas. Tortoises are a type of turtle that mostly live on land, in deserts, grasslands, and forests.

WHAT IT EATS

The painted turtle is an **omnivore** and eats a mix of plants like grasses, leaves, and fruits, and invertebrates like insects, snails, and worms.

FUN FACT

The giant tortoise is a type of turtle that can live for 200 years!

egg

QUICK FACTS

Most common species: American Toad
Animal type: Amphibian
Activity time: Daytime (diurnal)

FROG & TOAD

Frogs and toads are amphibians. They can live both on water and land. They are often confused for one another, but they do have differences. Frogs have longer back legs made for jumping, while toads have shorter, stubbier back legs meant for hopping or walking. Frogs spend their lives living close to water while most toads prefer dry land.

Frogs have skin that is smooth and moist, while toads have skin that is dry and rough. Frogs can be green, yellow, brown, and gray, and can be quite colorful. Toads, on the other hand, are usually brownish-green with dark spots. Frogs are slimmer, while toads tend to be chubbier.

tadpole

SIZE

American toads are usually 2 to 3.5 inches long. The smallest toad in North America is the oak toad—it grows to only 1.3 inches in length.

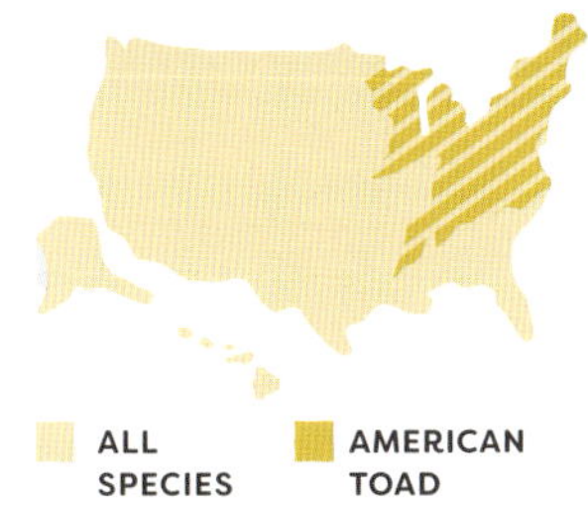

HABITAT & RANGE

Frogs and toads are found all over the world except in the coldest areas. Frogs like to live near bodies of fresh water, like ponds, lakes, rivers, and marshes. They need moisture to prevent dehydration and for laying eggs. Toads are better able to live in drier areas and are often found in woodlands, grasslands, gardens, and even sometimes deserts. Most species also need water for laying eggs, but not for day-to-day survival.

WHAT IT EATS

Frogs and toads both eat many types of insects. Larger types of frogs can also eat small fish, birds, and even some of the smallest mammals. They both catch food by sticking out their long tongues to catch their **prey**.

FUN FACT

All toads are frogs, but not all frogs are toads!

QUICK FACTS

Most common species: Mudpuppy
Animal type: Amphibian
Activity time: Nighttime (nocturnal)

SALAMANDER

Salamanders are amphibians, known for their smooth skin and long, slim bodies. Although they are not reptiles, they are often confused with lizards. Unlike lizards, salamanders have moist, not dry, skin. They also don't have claws like lizards do, as they don't do much digging. There are over 200 types of salamanders in North America. The most common is called a mudpuppy.

Salamanders have smooth, moist skin in different colors depending on the species—they can be shades of brown, green, red, and yellow, and some have patterns. They have long bodies, short legs, and long tails.

SIZE

Salamanders vary in size, but most adults are between 4 and 6 inches long. Mudpuppies, however, grow quite large, to 8 to 19 inches long.

larva

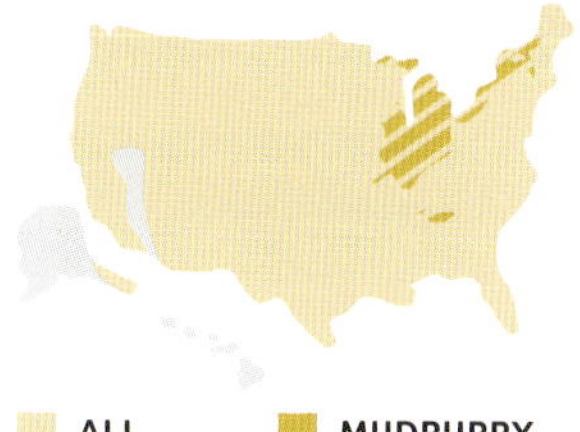

HABITAT & RANGE

Salamanders live all over North America, Europe, and Asia. They are usually found in moist environments, including forests, swamps, streams, and wetlands. They prefer **habitats** with leaf litter, rocks, and logs to tuck themselves beneath.

WHAT IT EATS

Salamanders are **carnivores**. Their diet mostly consists of insects, worms, small fish, snails, and spiders. Larger salamander species may also consume small animals.

FUN FACT

Some salamanders, especially the brightly colored ones, are poisonous.

QUICK FACTS

Most common species: Pavement Ant
Animal type: Invertebrate
Activity time: Daytime (diurnal)

ANT

Ants are very social insects known for their incredible teamwork. They build and live in highly organized colonies. Each **colony**, or community, usually has a queen or multiple queens who lay eggs. There are also worker ants who gather food, care for the young, and protect the colony. Some species also have soldier ants that defend the nest. Ants communicate with each other using chemicals, which they use to leave trails, signal danger, and organize tasks.

Ants can be black, brown, yellow, or red. They have three separate sections that make up their bodies—the head, thorax, and abdomen. They also have **antennae** that bend in the middle, similar to a human arm.

SIZE

Depending on the species, an ant's size will vary. They range in length from 0.08 inch to 1 inch in length. Pavement ants are about the size of a grain of rice!

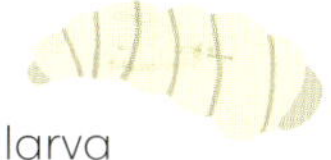
larva

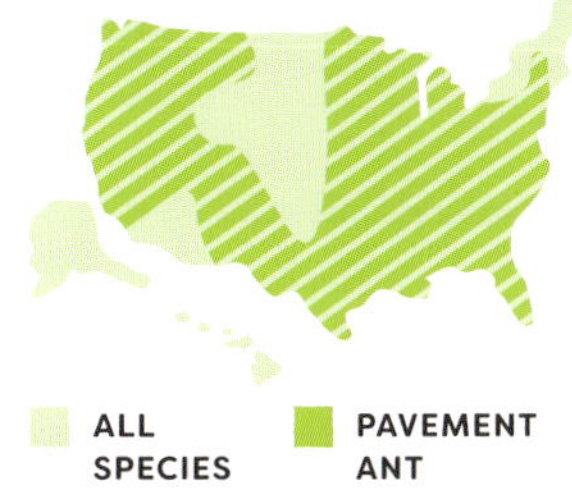

HABITAT & RANGE

Ants are found all over the world and in many **habitats**. Some kinds of ants, such as carpenter ants, prefer to live in an area with lots of trees. Others, like Pharaoh ants, prefer living in warm areas like houses, close to a rich food source like a family's kitchen.

WHAT IT EATS

Ants are **omnivores**. Many ants are attracted to sweet foods, such as nectar and fruits. Sometimes ants eat other insects, dead animals, and even a type of plant matter called fungi (mushrooms), to get protein in their diet.

FUN FACT

Adult ants don't eat solid food. Instead, they store it in a pocket in the back of their jaws. There, saliva breaks the food down. The liquid is swallowed and any remaining bits are spit out.

QUICK FACTS

Most common species: Common Eastern Bumblebee
Animal type: Invertebrate
Activity time: Daytime (diurnal)

BUMBLEBEE

Bumblebees are social insects known for their important role in pollination. In the spring, summer, and fall they visit flowers, gathering nectar and spreading pollen. They live in **colonies**, usually consisting of a queen bee, worker bees, and drones (male bees). Like honeybees, bumblebees have stingers, but they don't usually sting unless they are threatened.

Bumblebees are black with yellow or orange bands. They have chunky, fuzzy bodies with two large eyes and three smaller eyes on the tops of their heads. On their back legs, they have a pollen basket, a place to store pollen as they collect it.

SIZE

Bumblebees typically range in size from 0.6 inch to 1 inch in length. Queens are the largest, followed by workers and then drones, which tend to be the smallest.

larvae in cluster of wax cells

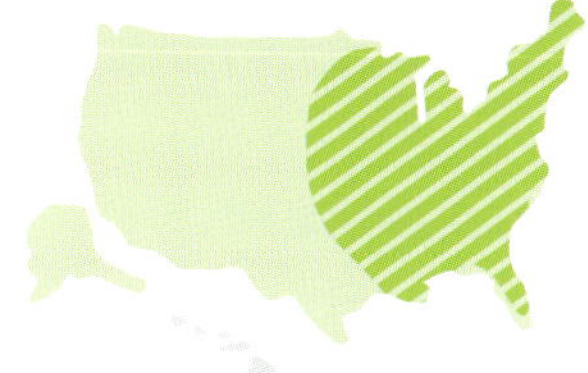

ALL SPECIES

COMMON EASTERN BUMBLEBEE

HABITAT & RANGE

Bumblebees can be found in much of the world, especially where the temperatures are mild. They make their nests in the ground, in nests abandoned by birds or other animals, and even sometimes in the sides of houses. They can be found in meadows, forests, gardens, and agricultural fields where flowering crops are grown.

WHAT IT EATS

Bumblebees mostly feed on nectar and pollen from flowering plants. Bumblebees have specialized mouths that allow them to reach nectar deep within flowers.

FUN FACT

One type of bumblebee called the cuckoo bumblebee sneaks into a nest and lays eggs, tricking the worker bees into caring for their young.

QUICK FACTS

Most common species: Cabbage White
Animal type: Invertebrate
Activity time: Daytime (diurnal)

BUTTERFLY

Butterflies, known for their colorful wings and graceful flight, play an important role in nature by being **pollinators**. As they fly from plant to plant, they spread pollen, which allows plants to produce seeds and fruit. There are more than 700 species of butterfly in North America. The cabbage white is the most common.

Butterflies have two pairs of wings that are covered in scales. They have two **antennae** on their heads, which they use to sense their surroundings, detect smells, and help with balance while flying. Butterflies do not have mouths. Instead, they have a long tongue called a **proboscis** that allows them to drink nectar from flowers.

SIZE

Butterflies come in many different sizes. Most have a **wingspan** between 2 and 5 inches. The cabbage white has a wingspan that ranges from 1.25 to 1.75 inches.

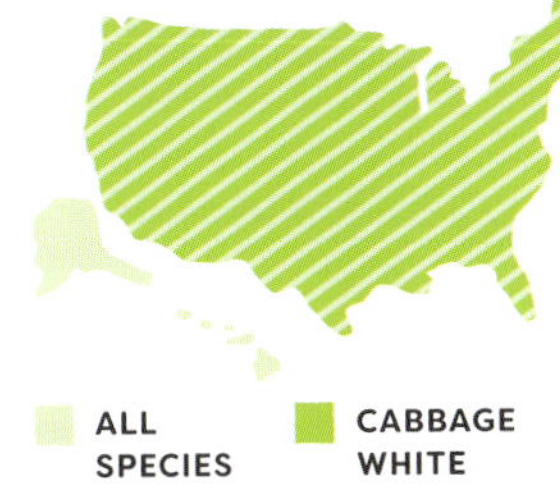

HABITAT & RANGE

Butterflies can live in many different environments, depending on the species. They are found all over the world, except in Antarctica. Meadows, forests, grasslands, wetlands, and even deserts are common **habitats** for butterflies.

WHAT IT EATS

Butterflies love to drink the sweet nectar from flowers, which gives them energy. They are also known to dine on rotting fruit, tree sap, and animal waste (yuck!).

FUN FACT

Butterflies taste with their feet! Taste receptors in their feet help them decide if a plant they've landed on is a good place to lay eggs.

QUICK FACTS
Most common species: Common Green Darner
Animal type: Invertebrate
Activity time: Daytime (diurnal)

DRAGONFLY

Dragonflies are a familiar sight in the summer. They zip around like helicopters in the air. They can even hover in midair! There are about 2,500 different species of dragonfly. In North America, the most common dragonfly is the common green darner.

Dragonflies are colorful insects, with bodies of blue, copper, green, or purple. They have thin bodies, two sets of wings, and giant eyes that almost touch.

SIZE

A dragonfly's body is usually about 3 inches long. Its wings are between 2 and 5 inches in length.

HABITAT & RANGE

Dragonflies live all over the world. The only landmass you will not find them on is Antarctica. They live near fresh water, and need it to complete their life cycle. Adult dragonflies lay their eggs in or near a body of water. The eggs hatch in about 7 days. The larvae will then spend the next few years underwater. There, they will hunt insects, mosquito larvae, and small fish.

WHAT IT EATS

Dragonflies mainly eat mosquitoes, flies, and other flying insects. They are excellent at controlling populations of pests.

FUN FACT

Dragonflies have six legs that they use as a basket to scoop up insects from the air before eating them.

QUICK FACTS

Most common species: Red-Legged Grasshopper
Animal type: Invertebrate
Activity time: Daytime (diurnal)

GRASSHOPPER

There are about 18,000 different kinds of grasshoppers in the world and they are all excellent jumpers. They use their jumping skills to get away from **predators**. Grasshoppers have very strong jaws and can destroy crops by eating their way through huge quantities of plants. You definitely don't want grasshoppers in your garden.

The red-legged grasshopper, the most common kind of grasshopper in North America, is named for its red hind legs. Its stomach is a greenish-yellow color and its back is reddish-brown.

SIZE

Female grasshoppers, at 0.7 to 1.2 inches long, are slightly larger than males.

HABITAT & RANGE

Grasshoppers live in a variety of climates, including deserts, mountains, and tropical forests. Some can even live in water! They are the most common in dry areas that have lots of grass and plants for them to eat.

WHAT IT EATS

Most grasshoppers are **herbivores**. Their diet consists of eating grasses. A few species of grasshopper will also eat some animal matter.

FUN FACT

If a grasshopper senses danger, it may puke up smelly vomit to keep a predator away.

QUICK FACTS

Most common species: Convergent Ladybug
Animal type: Invertebrate
Activity time: Daytime (diurnal)

LADYBUG

Colorful, cute, and totally harmless, ladybugs are thought to be a sign of good luck. They are active in spring, summer, and fall. In the winter, they **hibernate** in **colonies**, sometimes with thousands of other ladybugs. They are useful in gardens, as they eat the pest bugs that can destroy plants.

Most commonly, ladybugs are red with black spots, but some are orange, yellow, brown, or black. They have oval-shaped bodies and black heads.

SIZE

These small insects are only 0.3 to 0.4 inches in length.

HABITAT & RANGE

Ladybugs can live in many different **habitats**. They are seen in cities, suburbs, forests, and near rivers.

WHAT IT EATS

They eat other insects and insect eggs. Farmers sometimes buy and release ladybugs to help keep unwanted pests under control.

FUN FACT

A single ladybug can eat up to 5,000 insects in its life!

QUICK FACTS

Most common species: Common Pill Woodlouse
Animal type: Invertebrate
Activity time: Daytime (diurnal)

ROLY POLY (PILL BUG)

Pill bugs, also known as roly polies, are small bugs best known for rolling into a tight ball when frightened. They do this to protect themselves from **predators**. Pill bugs are **scavengers** and they help gardens and forests by eating rotting plant matter and improving the soil. You are most likely to find them hiding under rocks, logs, and leaves.

Most pill bugs are gray or dark brown. They are oval shaped with overlapping plates that look like armor. They have seven pairs of legs and two small **antennae**. They look like tiny armadillos!

SIZE

Pill bugs are small, only about 0.7 inches long. That's about the width of a dime.

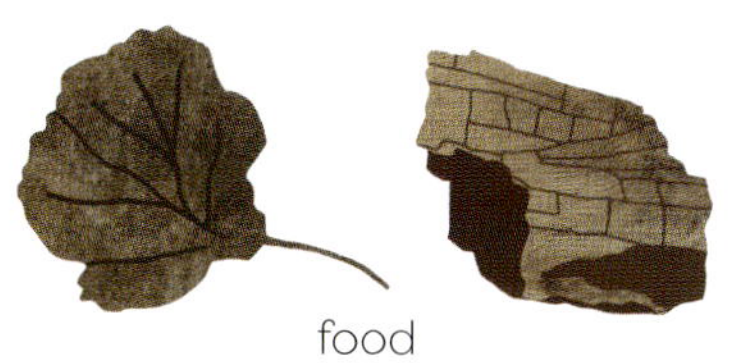

food

ALL SPECIES

COMMON PILL WOODLOUSE

HABITAT & RANGE

Pill bugs can be found in gardens, flowerbeds, and forests all over the world.

WHAT IT EATS

Pill bugs eat decaying plant material. They rarely eat live plants, but may nibble on roots or seedlings if there are no rotting leaves or wood to enjoy.

FUN FACT

Pill bugs have lots of nicknames. In addition to being called roly-polies, they are also referred to as potato bugs, doodle bugs, leg pebbles, and armadillo bugs.

QUICK FACTS

Most common species: Common Garden Snail
Animal type: Invertebrate
Activity time: Daytime (diurnal)

SNAIL

There are many species of snails, some of which live near water and others on land. They are known for their coiled shells, which help keep them safe. They are very slow moving and leave a trail of slime wherever they go.

Snails have soft bodies with a "foot," or flat muscle, that helps them glide over surfaces. On their heads they have two pairs of tentacles, one of which has a pair of eyes. A snail's spiral shell can vary in size, shape, and color depending on the species.

food

SIZE

Snails vary in size. The common garden snail is 1 to 1.5 inches long, including its body and shell.

ALL SPECIES

COMMON GARDEN SNAIL

HABITAT & RANGE

Many snail species live in gardens, forests, and grasslands, where they can find plenty of plant material for food and moist conditions to prevent drying out. Aquatic snails live in ponds, lakes, streams, and oceans.

WHAT IT EATS

Most snails eat plant material, like leaves, stems, and decaying organic matter. They use a special organ called a radula to eat. The radula is a ribbon-like structure covered in tiny teeth that they use to scrape food from surfaces.

FUN FACT

Snails and slugs are almost exactly the same, except that snails have shells and slugs do not.

QUICK FACTS

Most common species: American House Spider
Animal type: Invertebrate
Activity time: Daytime (diurnal)

SPIDER

order Araneida

Spiders are perhaps best known for spinning webs and scaring people! Although many people are scared of spiders, most species are harmless to humans. There are many different types of spiders—more than 46,700 species all over the world. They are helpful to have around, as they eat other harmful insects. Spiders are not actually insects—they are **arachnids**, like ticks, mites, and scorpions.

Most spiders have eight legs, eight eyes, and silk glands on their stomachs that allow them to spin silk.

SIZE

Spider sizes vary greatly depending on the species. House spiders that you may have seen in your home can range from 0.1 inch (teeny tiny) to a half inch long.

HABITAT & RANGE

Spiders can be found in nearly every **habitat** on Earth. They are commonly found in forests, grasslands, urban areas, inside homes, and even underwater!

WHAT IT EATS

Spiders are **carnivores** and mostly eat insects. Most spiders are happy to gobble flies, mosquitoes, ants, and other small insects. Some, like the black widow, prey on other spiders. Larger spiders, like tarantulas, may eat small mammals, lizards, or frogs. Spiders mostly catch meals in their webs, but some species, like the wolf spider, stalk and pounce on their **prey**.

FUN FACT

Female spiders tend to be much larger than males. This is unusual in the animal world.

QUICK FACTS
Most common species: Earthworm
Animal type: Invertebrate
Activity time: Daytime (diurnal)

WORM

When you think of worms, what words come to mind? These slippery, slithery, wiggly, crawly creatures might not seem very important, but they are! Worms play a large part in keeping soil healthy. As they crawl through the dirt, the spaces they make bring air to the soil. They eat dead stuff and their poop acts as **fertilizer.** They help to keep a healthy balance of water in the earth. We have a lot to thank worms for!

Worms are long and thin, with no limbs. They can be brown or dark gray, but some species can even be green or pink. Worm eggs develop in protective casings called cocoons, then hatch out of them and live in the soil.

cocoon

SIZE

Worms can be vastly different sizes depending on the species. The earthworm is usually only a few inches in length, but can grow to up to 14 inches long.

HABITAT & RANGE

Different species of worm can live in different **habitats**. The earthworm is found in North America, Europe, and Asia. They enjoy soil that has some moisture and lots of decaying matter to eat.

WHAT IT EATS

Earthworms eat soil and anything that's in the soil. That includes dead leaves, bug poop, bacteria, small insects, and grass.

FUN FACT

There is a type of worm called the beard worm. True to its name, it has about 200,000 hairlike tentacles.

MY ANIMAL LOG

Here you can keep track of all the backyard animals you have spotted. In the Notes column, add details about the animal's appearance or behavior.

NAME OF ANIMAL	DATE	LOCATION	NOTES

NAME OF ANIMAL	DATE	LOCATION	NOTES

CONSERVATION

Protecting backyard animals, insects, and birds is important for maintaining a healthy, balanced **ecosystem**. Here are some reasons to support and protect them:

→ A diverse range of species in your backyard helps create a balanced environment. Each species plays a specific role, contributing to a healthy **ecosystem**.

→ Observing and protecting backyard wildlife offers hands-on learning experiences for children and adults alike. Watching birds, insects, and other animals in their natural behavior can help foster curiosity, respect, and a deeper understanding of nature.

→ Many backyard insects, such as bees, butterflies, and beetles, are **pollinators**. Pollinators play a part in food production. Many plants need to be pollinated in order to make fruit, vegetables, and flowers.

→ Some insects, like ladybugs and spiders, help control pest populations. Natural pest control without chemicals is much better for the environment and all living things.

→ Worms, beetles, ants, and pill bugs help keep soil healthy. They bring nutrients and air to the soil so that it is healthier for growing plants.

→ Interacting with nature and being outside has been shown to reduce stress and improve mood. Even just observing birds and insects in your backyard can increase well-being.

GLOSSARY

adaptable Able to change to suit other environments and conditions.

antennae The parts of an insect that are used for smell or to help feel what's around them.

arachnid A class of animals that includes spiders.

buck A male deer.

burrow Underground tunnels dug by animals for them to live in.

camouflage The act of blending into surroundings to hide.

carnivore An animal that eats meat.

carrion Meat from a dead animal.

colony A group of insects living in a dwelling together.

diurnal Active during the daytime.

doe A female deer.

domesticated Adapted to live with humans.

ecosystem All of the living things in an area.

fertilizer Something added to soil to give it nutrients.

habitat The natural home of a plant or animal.

herbivore An animal that only eats plants.

hibernate To spend time being inactive, usually in the winter.

marsupial An animal that carries its young in a pouch.

migrate Moving from one area to another.

native Growing or living naturally in a particular place.

nocturnal Active at night.

omnivore Eating both plants and animals.

pollinator An insect that does the work of moving pollen to help a plant reproduce.

predator An animal that lives by killing and eating another animal.

prey An animal that is hunted and killed by another animal.

proboscis An insect's tubular sucking mouthpiece.

scavenger An animal that feeds on waste material, carrion, or dead plant matter.

tundra A flat, treeless Arctic region where parts of the soil are permanently frozen.

vegetation Plant life.

venomous Able to inject toxins into a victim, usually through a bite or sting.

wingspan The distance between the wing tips of a winged animal.

First Edition
30 29 28 27 26 5 4 3 2 1

Published by
Gibbs Smith
570 N. Sportsplex Drive
Kaysville, Utah 84037
www.gibbs-smith.com
The authorized representative in the EEA is Simon and Schuster Netherlands BV, Herculesplein 96 3584 AA Utrecht, Netherlands, info@simonandschuster.nl

Designed by Renee Bond
Manufactured in Dongguan Guangdong, China, in November 2025 by RR Donnelley Asia Printing Solutions.

Library of Congress Control Number: 2025938690
ISBN: 978-1-4236-6886-2

This product is made of FSC®-certified and other controlled material.

SCRIPTURAL NOVENA TO JESUS IN THE BLESSED SACRAMENT

Jesus, I adore you.

Scriptural Novena to Jesus in the Blessed Sacrament

Most Rev. Arthur J. Serratelli
S.T.D., S.S.L., D.D.

CATHOLIC BOOK PUBLISHING CORP.
New Jersey

NIHIL OBSTAT: Rev. T. Kevin Corcoran, MA., S.T.B.
Censor Librorum

IMPRIMATUR: ✠ Most Rev. David M. O'Connell, C.M., J.C.D., D.D.
Bishop of Trenton

January 9, 2022
Baptism of the Lord

The Nihil Obstat and Imprimatur are official declarations that a book or pamphlet is free of doctrinal or moral error. No implication is contained therein that those who have granted the Nihil Obstat and Imprimatur agree with the contents, opinions or statements expressed.

(T-948)

ISBN 978-1-953152-82-4

Totowa, NJ 07512
Printed in Korea 22 NT 1
catholicbookpublishing.com

Contents

Introduction

On the ancient Via Salaria that leads north out of Rome are the Catacombs of Priscilla. One of Rome's oldest catacombs, these catacombs are well known for their religious frescoes. Among these are Abraham's sacrifice of Isaac, the Good Shepherd, the Final Judgment and what is considered the earliest depiction of the Madonna with Child. In the Capella Greca, there is the famous "*Fractio Panis*" (The Breaking of the Bread).

Dated to the first half of the 2nd century A.D., this fresco depicts six men and one woman reclining at a meal. On the table are two large plates. One plate contains two fish; the other, five loaves. On either side of the table are baskets filled with loaves. The fresco is the earliest artistic representation of Jesus' miracle of the multiplication of loaves and fish. But there is more.

At one end of the table, a bearded man, somewhat apart from the others, is depicted "breaking bread." This action Acts of the Apostles uses to designate the Eucharist (Acts 2:42; 20:7). In order to make sure anyone viewing this fresco would understand

this, the artist placed in front of the man breaking bread a two-handled cup, the type of chalice used in the 2nd century celebration of the Eucharist. The artist wants us to see Jesus' miracle of the multiplication of the loaves and fish as a type and symbol of the Eucharist.

On Rome's Via Appia Antica are the Catacombs of St. Callistus. In the most ancient part of these catacombs, in the crypt of Lucina, there is a fresco depicting two baskets on a green field. One basket has fish; the other, bread. In each there is a striking and unexpected detail. The artist has placed in each basket a glass of red wine. By depicting bread and wine, the basic elements of the Eucharist, in a fresco of the multiplication of loaves and fish, the artist is reminding us that the miracle Jesus performed for the thousands one day in Galilee was just a foretaste of the greater miracle of feeding the more than thousands with His Body and Blood in the Eucharist throughout the centuries to follow.

Many early Christian writers such as Origen (*In Matt.*, x, 25) and Ambrose (*De Virgin.*, I, 3) likewise saw this connection of the multiplication of the loaves and fish with the Eucharist. But this is no surprise.

The four evangelists themselves had already made the connection in their gospels.

When recording the multiplication of the loaves and fish, Matthew, Mark and Luke all use the exact same words for the miracle. Jesus "took" the bread, "blessed" it, "broke" it and "gave" it to the disciples (Mt 14:19; Mk 6:41; Lk 9:16). Matthew and Mark use these very same words to record Jesus' giving of the Eucharist (Mt 26:26; Mk 14:23). Obviously for them, something of the meaning of the Eucharist is already contained in the miracle.

In Luke's account of the Last Supper, the evangelist does not say Jesus "blessed" (εὐλογεῖν: *eulogein*) the bread as he does in the multiplication of the loaves and fish. Instead, Luke says Jesus took the bread and "gave thanks" (εὐχαριστειν: *eucharistein*, Lk 22:19). However, in terms of how Jesus is praying in working the miracle and in giving the Eucharist, both "to bless" and "to give thanks" have the same meaning. For Luke, as for Matthew and Mark, the miracle of the multiplication of the loaves points to the Eucharist.

John does not record the institution of the Eucharist as does the other evangelists. By the time he is writing his gospel, the Church is celebrating the Eucharist, repeating the words Jesus used at the Last Supper.

Instead of repeating what the first three evangelists tell us, John chooses to relate Jesus' Bread of Life Discourse in the synagogue of Capernaum. In this discourse, Jesus unequivocally explains that we receive His Body and Blood as the Bread of Life. John places this discourse immediately after the miracle of the loaves and fish. Like the other evangelists, John connects the miracle with the Eucharist. He hints at this connection when he tells us that, in the multiplying of the bread, Jesus took the bread and "gave thanks" (εὐχαριστειν: *eucharistein*, Jn 6:11).

Furthermore, the gospel writers by their choice of certain words color their accounts of the multiplication of the loaves and fish with Eucharistic overtones. They speak of the fragments (κλάσματα: *klasmata*) that were left over. This is the very same word that the *Didache*, the oldest Patristic writing from about 90 A.D., uses for the bread broken and consecrated at the Eucharist (*Didache* 9, 3.4).

In addition, in all gospels, the disciples collect the fragments that are left over (Mt 14:20; Mk 6:43; Lk 9:17; Jn 6:13). They do this in obedience to Jesus who commands them, "Gather up the fragments that are left over so that nothing will be wasted [perish]" (Jn 6:12). From the very beginning, the

Church had such reverence for the Eucharist that even the small particles of the Eucharist were carefully guarded.

Origen instructed those receiving Holy Communion, telling them, "When you receive the Body of the Lord, you are to preserve it with all care and veneration, lest the smallest particle of it should fall" (Origen, *Hom.* 13 *in Exodus*, n.3). In like manner, St. Cyril of Jerusalem said, "Partake of it [the Eucharist], giving heed lest you lose any part of it" (St. Cyril, *Catechetical Lectures*, XXIII, n.21-22). The 5th century Bishop Rabula of Edessa showed the same respect for the Eucharist. He said, "Let any crumb of the holy Body which falls to the ground be carefully searched for."

The fact that the Eucharist is at the heart of the Church may very well be the reason why the evangelists give the miracle of the loaves and fish such a prominent place in their gospels. It is the only miracle that Jesus performed that is recorded in all four gospels. Each gospel records the miracle of Jesus' multiplying bread and fish for the 5,000 (Mt 14:13-21; Mk 6:31-44; Lk 9:12-17; Jn 6:1-14). And two gospels also narrate His multiplying bread and fish for the 4,000 ((Mt 15:32-39; Mk 8:1-9).

Some scholars question whether the six accounts of the miracle of the multiplication of loaves and bread all refer to one and the same event. They suggest that perhaps the same miracle is simply preserved in two different traditions. What can be said?

Jesus healed many invalids. He gave sight to more than one blind man. He cured many sick. He raised the daughter of Jairus, the only son of the widow of Nain and His beloved friend Lazarus from the dead. There is no reason to exclude the possibility that He miraculously fed the crowds that followed Him on two separate occasions. However, our primary task in interpreting the sacred page is to uncover what the evangelists are telling us in giving us both accounts.

The feeding of the 5,000 takes place near Bethsaida, close to the Sea of Galilee. This is distinctly Jewish territory and the twelve apostles who assist Jesus are all Jewish. This narrative, then, reveals Jesus as the Bread of Life for Jewish Christians.

The second miracle of feeding the 4,000 takes place in the region around the Decapolis, the territory of the Gentiles. Seven disciples assist Jesus. They most likely represent the seven Greek-speaking deacons

of the primitive community. This second miracle reminds us that all—Greeks as well as Jews—are invited to the banquet of the Body and Blood of Jesus. Jesus is the Bread of Life for everyone. No one is excluded.

The four evangelists understood that, when Jesus multiplied the loaves of bread in the bright sunshine of the Galilee, He meant that miracle to shed light on how we understand, celebrate and live the Eucharist. In the following pages, we will look at and meditate on various aspects of the first miracle of the multiplication of the loaves and fish in order to grow in our appreciation and love of the Eucharist. Each reflection is meant to lead us to adore Jesus truly present in the Blessed Sacrament.

Eucharistic Adoration belongs to the heart of Catholic piety. As St. Augustine strongly encourages us, "No one eats this flesh unless he has first adored . . . we would sin by not adoring" (St. Augustine, *Enarratio in* Ps. 98, 9). In our acts of thanksgiving, reparation, petition, and adoration before the Blessed Sacrament, we deepen our union with Jesus and come to taste already the joy of the eternal banquet that awaits us in heaven.

First Day

The Compassion of Jesus

"When he came ashore and saw the vast crowd, he had compassion on them..."
Mt 14: 14

C.S. Lewis once remarked that "what one calls interruptions are precisely one's real life—the life God is sending..." This is clearly evident in the miracle of the multiplication of loaves and fish. The people for whom Jesus works this miracle are actually interrupting His carefully planned ministry. Yet it is a moment of great grace.

Jesus is at the height of His popularity. His teaching and miracles have attracted many. The crowds rush to sit at the feet of the Master and soak in His every word. They come bringing their sick and infirm to be healed and made whole. But their timing is inconvenient. Jesus is seeking a respite from His ministry.

The apostles have just completed their first mission on which Jesus sent them. They are full of wonder and joy. Flushed with success, they cannot wait to tell Jesus what they had witnessed when they preached.

Jesus bids them, "Come away with me, by yourselves... and rest a while" (Mk 6:31). He recognizes their need for physical rest after their arduous missionary journeys. He knows their deeper need to be with Him. For any effort apart from Jesus soon shrivels up and produces no good fruit. Only in constant communion with Jesus can our good works bring God's healing to others.

At this moment, not just the apostles but even Jesus Himself needs a respite from the multitudes. At the behest of Salome, King Herod has beheaded John the Baptist. His disciples bury his body and flee to Jesus. John had prepared the way. On the banks of the Jordan, he had pointed Jesus out as the Messiah and now John is gone. The death of the Baptist brings his disciples to the Lord. John's disciples are ready to give their allegiance to Jesus. Any loss can become a gain when it leads us to Christ.

Jesus had great respect for John. He once said to the crowds, "Amen, I say to you, among those born of women, no one has been greater than John the Baptist" (Mt 11:11). He even had insisted that John baptize Him when He began His public ministry. John never wavered from his role as precursor.

His sole mission was to lead others to Christ. Even his death brings others to Jesus.

The news of John's death at the hands of the cruel tyrant Herod saddens Jesus. Jesus wept at the tomb of his friend Lazarus. At the death of the Baptist, the Man of sorrows now longs for the solitude to shed His silent tears.

Matthew tells us that "When Jesus received this news [of John's death], he withdrew ...in a boat by himself to a deserted place" (Mt 14:13). The word "withdraw" (ἀναχωρέω: *anachoreo*) which Matthew uses here to speak of Jesus' seeking to be alone, Matthew uses elsewhere in his gospel to indicate the need to escape from imminent danger.

To avoid the evil plans of Herod, the Magi "departed (literally, they withdrew—ἀνεχώρησαν: *anechōrēsan*) for their own country" (Mt 2:12). To keep Herod from killing the infant Jesus, Joseph took Mary and Jesus and departed (literally, withdrew—ἀνεχώρησεν: *anechōrēsen*) from Bethlehem (Mt 2:14). On returning from Egypt, in order to protect Jesus from Herod's cruel and vicious son Archelaus, Joseph "withdrew to the region of Galilee" (Mt 2:22).

"When Jesus learned that John had been arrested, He withdrew to Galilee" (Mt 4:12). After Jesus healed the man with a withered hand, the Pharisees began to plot to put Jesus to death. "When Jesus became aware of this, he departed (literally, withdrew—ἀνεχώρησεν: *anechōrēsen*) from that place" (Mt 12:15). In each of these instances, Matthew uses the word "withdraw" (ἀναχωρέω: *anachóreó*) to speak of moving out of harm's way.

Death has silenced the Baptist. Jesus knows that Herod is looking for a way to do away with Him. He escapes to a deserted place not because He fears death. Rather, His hour has not yet come. Prudence dictates that we do everything possible not to hasten the moment of our demise. Jesus has much yet to do to usher in the kingdom and He will not let the political ambitions of a self-serving leader stop Him.

To find a quiet place for Himself and His apostles away from the crowds, Jesus crosses the Sea of Galilee in a boat. "But when the people learned of it, they followed him on foot from the towns. When he came ashore and saw the vast crowd, he had compassion on them…" (Mt 14:13-14; also Mk 6:34). A

lesser person would have been annoyed. But not Jesus!

His time to attend to the needs of His apostles and His own sorrow are being snatched from Him. Yet His response is the noblest. His personal grief for the dead yields to compassion for the living. Not the slightest sigh of disappointment. Not a single word of rebuke to the crowds. Jesus puts aside His own good for the good of the many. After teaching the crowds and healing the sick among them, Jesus sees the need for the famished crowd to eat. Nothing escapes His notice. The same compassion that led Him to teach and heal now leads Him to work the miracle of the multiplication of loaves and fish (Jn 6:5).

The Greek word σπλαγχνίζομαι [*splagchnizomai*] used to speak of Jesus being moved with compassion is a most remarkable word. It is not found in classic Greek. It is not found in the Septuagint, i.e. the Greek Old Testament. But the word is found three times on the lips of Jesus: in the parables of the Unforgiving Servant, the Good Samaritan, and the Prodigal Son. For Jesus, God is compassionate. Most likely the evangelists, remembering Jesus' teaching, coined

the Greek word for compassion to hint at Jesus' own divinity.

Luke captures Jesus' compassionate response to those who interrupt His rest, hungering for truth and longing for healing. Luke tells us, "Jesus welcomed them and spoke to them about the kingdom of God. He also cured those who were in need of healing" (Lk 9:11). The word "welcome" (ἀποδέχομαι: *apodechomai*) is unique to Luke. More than just a self-sacrificing cordiality, it implies the joy of being able to do good. Jesus finds His joy in leading us to the happiness of being one with God.

Jesus Christ who welcomed all who came to Him, no matter the hour or the motive, will never turn us away. "The Son of Man came to seek out and to save what was lost" (Lk 19:10). Jesus stays with us in the Eucharist. It is the sacrament of Divine compassion. Whether it is a physical, emotional, or spiritual need that brings us before Jesus in the Blessed Sacrament, He greets us with open arms and embraces us in love. The closer we come to the Lord, the greater our joy.

The fruit of love is service, which is compassion in action.

St. Teresa of Calcutta

PRAYERS

O God, come to my assistance.
O Lord, make haste to help me.

Glory be to the Father, and to the Son
And to the Holy Spirit.
As it was in the beginning is now
and ever shall be, world without end. Amen.

Prayer for the First Day

Most Merciful Jesus, whose very nature it is to have compassion on us and to forgive us, do not look upon our sins but upon our trust which we place in Your infinite goodness. Receive us into the abode of Your Most Compassionate Heart, and never let us escape from it. We beg this of You by the love which unites You to the Father and the Holy Spirit.

Eternal Father, turn Your merciful gaze upon us poor sinners, enfolded in the Most Compassionate Heart of Jesus. For the sake of His sorrowful Passion show us Your mercy, that we may praise You who live and reign forever and ever. Amen.

Prayer of Adoration

Lord Jesus Christ, I adore and I worship You present in the Blessed Sacrament. I

thank You for Your great love in giving us Your very Body and Blood, Soul and Divinity in the Eucharist. I truly believe that You are present in this great Sacrament of the Altar. Night and day, You remain with us, drawing us closer to Your Most Sacred Heart, full of compassion and mercy for us poor sinners. I offer You all my thoughts, words, deeds, and affections. Graciously accept the homage of my life. By the grace of the Holy Spirit, make me love You more and more so that I may love all others in Your Name and be pleasing to the Father. You who live and reign forever and ever. Amen.

Prayer of Petition

Father Most Merciful, I praise and thank You for the gift of Jesus, Your only begotten Son whom You sent as our Savior and Redeemer. I truly believe that Jesus who remains with us in the Most Blessed Sacrament of the Altar stands before Your throne of grace, making constant intercession for us. In His outstretched hands, I place my fervent prayer (*here mention your intentions*). Have mercy on me and answer me according to Your holy will. With full confidence in Your kindness, I offer my prayer in the Name of Jesus who lives and

reigns with You in the unity of the Holy Spirit, God, forever and ever. Amen.

Prayer to Our Blessed Mother

O Mary, most blessed of all women, to you we come in humble petition. From you, Virgin Immaculate, the Son of God took flesh and became our Savior. By His Suffering, Death, and Resurrection, He has won for us the forgiveness of our sins and the gift of eternal life. Mother of the Redeemer, look with pity on us, and help us grow in a greater and greater devotion to the Eucharist, the very Body and Blood, Soul and Divinity of your beloved Son. Through your powerful intercession, Refuge of sinners, gain for us true sorrow for our sins so that we may worthily share in the Eucharist, the Sacrifice of the Cross made present to us, and, with firm faith, receive Him in Holy Communion. Mother of Divine Grace, assist us with your prayers so that our whole lives become an act of adoration and praise of Jesus who is Lord forever and ever. Amen.

O Sacrament Most Holy,
O Sacrament Divine!
All praise and all thanksgiving
be every moment Thine.

For additional prayers see page 113

Second Day 2
Jesus the Good Shepherd

"The Lord is my shepherd; there is nothing I shall lack."

Ps 23:1

The Catacombs of St. Domitilla contain a fresco that is the earliest known depiction of Christ as the Good Shepherd. It dates back to the 2nd century. The image of the Good Shepherd was the most popular depiction of Jesus in the art of the catacombs. It is found in frescoes and on sarcophagi. This image traces its lineage to Jesus Himself.

Jesus used the metaphor of the shepherd to speak of Himself implicitly in the Parable of the Lost Sheep (Mt 18:12-14; Lk 15:3-7). Explicitly He identified Himself as the Good Shepherd in His discourse in the Gospel of John 10:1-18. In depicting Himself as the Good Shepherd, Jesus was drawing from the rich biblical tradition of His people.

The patriarchs Abraham, Isaac and Jacob were all shepherds. So were Moses and David. As these leaders cared for and protected their families, so does God look after His people. Quite naturally, therefore, the image of the

shepherd became a way of speaking about God and also about the Messiah.

On his deathbed, Jacob blessed his twelve sons, predicting the destiny of their progeny (Gen 49:2-27). Jacob praised God for guiding him, for being his God. He called him "the Shepherd, the Rock of Israel" (Gen 49:24). The psalmists echo Jacob's words when they address God as the "Shepherd of Israel" (Ps 80:2; 95:7).

Moses had been a shepherd. After he fled Egypt and Pharaoh's palace, he tended the flocks of his father-in-law Jethro in Midian. He knew how easily sheep can become disoriented and lost. While shepherding Israel through the Exodus, he came to see how much they were like sheep. They needed proper guidance so as not to wander aimlessly and confused.

When the people of Israel were poised to enter the Promised Land, God tells Moses that his death is imminent (Deut 32:48-52; Num 27:12-14). He would soon die without ever setting foot on the land God was giving to His people. Moses grieves not for himself. His thoughts turn immediately to the people whom he has been leading to the Promised Land. And he prays:

> May the Lord, the God of the spirits of all flesh, place a man over the assembly who will go out and come in before them, and who will lead them out and bring them in, so that the assembly of the Lord might not be like sheep without a shepherd.
>
> Num 27:15-17

In petitioning God for a worthy successor to lead the people out and bring them in, Moses is taking a metaphor from the way a shepherd cares for his flock in the Middle East. He goes before the sheep. He leads them forth to good pastures and then brings them back safely home.

Moses does not indulge in self-pity over his own fate. He is more concerned for the life of his people than his own death. Such self-forgetfulness is the sign of a truly noble person. He begs God for someone to succeed him who will be a good shepherd.

God grants his petition and appoints Joshua to shepherd Israel (Num 27:18). Joshua's name means "God is my salvation." This is the very same name that Jesus bore in His native Aramaic. "Jesus" is simply the Greek equivalent. Joshua led Israel in the final conquest of the Promised Land,

the home God had promised the patriarchs. Joshua is a type of the Messiah to come. For Jesus, anointed Messiah by God, conquers death and leads us into our true home in heaven. Jesus the Good Shepherd is God's final answer to Moses' prayer.

The prophet Micah was a contemporary of Isaiah. He lived in the turbulent days of the divided kingdom. Isaiah looked to Jerusalem for the coming of the Messiah. But not Micah. He turned his eyes away from the throne of David in Jerusalem to the small village of David's birth. He pointed to Bethlehem and said,

> But from you, O Bethlehem Ephrathah, among the tiniest of the clans of Judah, from you will come forth for me one who is to be ruler in Israel, one whose origins are from the distant past, from ancient times.....He will rise up to shepherd [the Lord's] flock.
>
> Mic 5:1-3

From Bethlehem would come the long-awaited Messiah who would shepherd Israel. In Micah's prophecy, the Hebrew verb *ra'ah* that translates "to shepherd" actually means "to feed" or "lead to pastures." Thus, the

Messiah will be a good shepherd who will provide ample food for God's people in good pastures. It is not surprising, therefore, that when Jesus feeds the crowds in the miracle of the multiplication of the loaves and fish, the gospel writers recognize Him as the shepherd who comes to care for God's people.

Both Matthew and Mark link Jesus' compassion on the crowds with His role as the Good Shepherd. When Jesus travels through the towns and villages and sees the crowds flock to Him, Matthew tells us that Jesus "had compassion on them because they were distressed and helpless like sheep without a shepherd" (Mt 9:36). Mark makes the same statement about Jesus in relating the miracle of the multiplication of loaves and fish. He says, "He had compassion on them, for they were like sheep without a shepherd" (Mk 6:34). Thus, Mark directly and Matthew indirectly see the miracle of the multiplication of loaves and fish as revealing Jesus' identity as the Good Shepherd. So also does John.

John together with Mark provides what seems to be a very insignificant detail when recounting the miracle. Mark tells us that, before multiplying the bread and fish, Jesus

orders the apostles "to have all the people sit down on the green grass…" (Mk 6:39). Almost as if in passing, John says the same thing. "Now there was plenty of grass in that place…" (Jn 6:10). Far from simply being the recollection of an eyewitness, this small detail of green grass is freighted with theological imagination. It indicates that both evangelists understand this miracle in light of Psalm 23, the most famous psalm about the Good Shepherd who feeds His flock in green pastures.

Indeed, the gospel texts of the miracle of the loaves and fish contain several allusions to Psalm 23. First, Jesus' making the people recline on the green grass (Mk 6:39; Jn 6:10) parallels Ps 23: 2: "He makes me lie down in green pastures." Second, Jesus' working this miracle close to the refreshing waters of the Sea of Galilee echoes Ps 23:2: "He leads me to tranquil streams [Hebrew: waters]."

Third, Jesus' teaching the crowds and healing their wearied bodies before multiplying the bread (Mt 14:14; Mk 6:34; Lk 9:11) parallels Ps 23:3: "He restores my soul, guiding me in paths of righteousness…" Fourth, Jesus provides more than the crowds can eat. "They all ate and were satisfied" (Mt 14:20; Mk 6:42;

Lk 9:17). Experiencing the abundant generosity of Jesus, each could say in the words of the psalmist, “There is nothing I shall lack” (Ps 23:1).

In Psalm 23, the Good Shepherd is God. In echoing this psalm in their account of the multiplication of loaves and fish, the gospel writers see this miracle as revealing the divinity of Jesus. It is by His power as God that He feeds the thousands. The narrative of the loaves and fish is not a parable about Jesus’ setting the example of sharing the little food He had and thus leading others to share their food with one another. It is not a lesson in selfless generosity. It is a genuine miracle of God’s creative power working in Jesus.

The prophet Ezekiel had said that one day God the Good Shepherd would gather His lost sheep and feed them on the mountains of Israel (Ezek 34:11-14). In the event of Jesus’ feeding the crowds in the multiplication of the loaves and fish, Jesus had come down the mountain. After the miracle, when they wanted to make Him king, “he again withdrew to the mountain by himself” (Jn 6:15). In Jesus the Good Shepherd on the mountain in Galilee, God Himself was caring for his flock. The gospel writers,

along with those present at the miracle, could truly exclaim, "The Lord is my shepherd" (Ps 23:1).

The meal Jesus provided in the desert place among the mountains of Israel was but a foretaste of the Eucharist. For in this great sacrament, the Good Shepherd provides for all our needs and always in abundance. As St. Paul says, He is "always at work within us to accomplish more than all we can ask or imagine" (Eph 3:20).

> *Is not our Lord as meek and humble in the Blessed Sacrament as He was during His life on earth? Is He not always the Good Shepherd, the Divine Consoler, the Changeless Friend? Happy the soul that knows how to find Jesus in the Holy Eucharist, and in the Eucharist all things!*
>
> St. Peter Julian Eymard

PRAYERS

O God, come to my assistance.
O Lord, make haste to help me.

Glory be to the Father, and to the Son
And to the Holy Spirit.
As it was in the beginning is now
and ever shall be, world without end. Amen.

Prayer for the Second Day

Lord Jesus present in the Eucharist, You are the Good Shepherd who never fails to feed Your flock. Lead me by the Holy Spirit into good pastures where You can nourish me by Your Presence and sustain me in the trials of life. Let your Body and Blood be for me a constant source of grace so that strengthened by You, I may willingly share Your love with all. You who live and reign with the Father and the Holy Spirit, God, forever and ever. Amen.

Prayer of Adoration

Lord Jesus Christ, I adore and I worship You present in the Blessed Sacrament. I thank You for Your great love in giving us Your very Body and Blood, Soul and Divinity in the Eucharist. I truly believe that You are present in this great Sacrament of the Altar. Night and day, You remain with us, drawing us closer to Your Most Sacred Heart, full of compassion and mercy for us poor sinners. I offer You all my thoughts, words, deeds, and affections. Graciously accept the homage of my life. By the grace of the Holy Spirit, make me love You more and more so that I may love all others in Your

Name and be pleasing to the Father. You who live and reign forever and ever. Amen.

Prayer of Petition

Father Most Merciful, I praise and thank You for the gift of Jesus, Your only begotten Son whom You sent as our Savior and Redeemer. I truly believe that Jesus who remains with us in the Most Blessed Sacrament of the Altar stands before Your throne of grace, making constant intercession for us. In His outstretched hands, I place my fervent prayer (*here mention your intentions*). Have mercy on me and answer me according to Your holy will. With full confidence in Your kindness, I offer my prayer in the Name of Jesus who lives and reigns with You in the unity of the Holy Spirit, God, forever and ever. Amen.

Prayer to Our Blessed Mother

O Mary, most blessed of all women, to you we come in humble petition. From you, Virgin Immaculate, the Son of God took flesh and became our Savior. By His Suffering, Death, and Resurrection, He has won for us the forgiveness of our sins and the gift of eternal life. Mother of the

Redeemer, look with pity on us and help us grow in a greater and greater devotion to the Eucharist, the very Body and Blood, Soul and Divinity of your beloved Son. Through your powerful intercession, Refuge of sinners, gain for us true sorrow for our sins so that we may worthily share in the Eucharist, the Sacrifice of the Cross made present to us, and, with firm faith, receive Him in Holy Communion. Mother of Divine Grace, assist us with your prayers so that our whole lives become an act of adoration and praise of Jesus who is Lord forever and ever. Amen.

O Sacrament Most Holy,
O Sacrament Divine!
All praise and all thanksgiving
be every moment Thine.

For additional prayers see page 113

Third Day

Jesus the New Moses

"The Lord your God will raise up from among your countrymen a prophet who will do what I have done for you, and you will listen to him."

Deut 18:15

When Moses was about to die, he comforted the people of Israel with the promise that God was not abandoning them. He prophesied that God would one day raise up a prophet who would lead them as he did. Moses literally described this future prophet as "a prophet like me" (Deut 18:15).

A long succession of prophets came after Moses. But these were not completely "like" Moses. They did not give a new law. They merely interpreted the Law which God gave Moses on Mt. Sinai. They did not inaugurate a new covenant. They only summoned the people to be faithful to the covenant which God had made with them through Moses.

Jesus alone fulfills the prophecy of Moses. He is truly "like" Moses in many ways. His very life parallels that of Moses. Herod the Great attempts to kill the infant Jesus just

as Pharaoh had issued a death warrant for the infant Moses. With signs and wonders, Moses had delivered the Israelites from bondage to Pharaoh. By His cross and resurrection, Jesus frees all people from slavery to sin and Satan.

Moses had ascended to Mt. Sinai to receive the Law from God. Jesus ascends the Mount of Beatitudes not to receive from God the new law of the kingdom, but to give that law with His own divine authority. Six times Jesus alludes to the Law of Moses by saying, "You have heard that it was said." Then He adds each time, "But I say to you."

Moses never said, "I say to you." He reported to the people "the words which the Lord had commanded him" (Ex 19:7). No prophet after Moses ever spoke on their own authority. They always announced that they were delivering to the people what God had commanded them to say. It was God's word, not theirs.

When Jesus says, "You have heard that it was said....But I say to you," He is not sweeping away the Old Law. Not at all! He is bringing it to fulfillment. He is deepening its meaning and demands. Moses laid down the Law in the name of God. But Jesus, the

Word Incarnate, speaks in His own name. Jesus is the New Moses who far surpasses Israel's greatest prophet.

In the miracle of multiplying the loaves and fish, the people recognize Jesus as the New Moses. The miracle takes place at the time of the Passover. Mark tells us that the grass was green (Mk 6:39). And, John says, "there was plenty of grass in that place" (Jn 6:10). Grass would not be green and plentiful except after April when the Jews would be celebrating the Passover. And John confirms this when he says, "The Jewish feast of Passover was approaching" (Jn 6:4).

The people who flock to Jesus have the Passover and the Exodus on their minds. Among them, some were on the way to Jerusalem for Passover. All of them were preparing for the feast that celebrates Moses' leading the people out of Egypt through the Red Sea across the desert to the Promised Land.

After wandering in the desert for thirty days, the Hebrews had become weary and tired. Their food supply was low. Their spirits even lower. Discontent is the slippery descent to disbelief. And so, facing the vast, unproductive desert of Sin, they forget all

the wonders God had done for them. Their faith weakens and they murmur.

> In the desert the entire community of the children of Israel murmured against Moses and Aaron. The children of Israel said to them, "Would that the hand of the Lord had killed us in the land of Egypt where we were seated by our pots filled with meat and where we had more than enough bread to eat. Instead you bought us out into this desert to slay the whole assembly with hunger.
>
> Ex 16:2-3

To their complaint, God responds with compassion. He rains down bread from heaven in the morning (Ex 16:4) and quail in the evening (Ex 16:13).

At the time of Jesus, the Jews remembered how God fed their ancestors in the desert. Their hearts burned with eager expectation for the prophet of the last days who would repeat what Moses did. There is a Palestinian midrash that captures this expectation.

> Rabbi Berachiah said in the name of Rabbi Isaac: The last redeemer will be like the first one. As it is said about the first one that "So Moses took his

> wife and his sons and set them on an ass" (Ex 4:20), so it is said about the last one "humble and riding on an ass" (Zech 9:9). As the first redeemer brought down the manna, as it is said "behold, I will rain bread from heaven for you" (Ex 16:4), so also the last redeemer will bring down the manna as it is said "the land will be covered with wheat" (Ps 72:16).
>
> Kohelet Rabbah, 1.1

Given their longing for a prophet just like Moses, there is no surprise at how the crowd reacts to Jesus' miracle of the loaves and fish. Almost instantly, when Jesus feeds the hungry crowds in the desert stretches of land around the Sea of Galilee, the people quickly rush to the judgment that Jesus is the prophet who is just like Moses. "When the people saw the sign he had performed, they began to say, 'This is indeed the prophet who is to come into the world'" (Jn 6:14).

The people were right; and, the apostles never forgot what they heard the people say that day. When Peter cures the lame man who was sitting and begging at the entrance to the Temple in Jerusalem, the people see him walking and leaping about in joy. They

are amazed and come running to see how this has happened (Acts 3:1-11). Peter seizes the opportunity to preach to them about Jesus. He speaks of Jesus' death and resurrection, telling the crowd that God had fulfilled in Jesus what He had promised through their prophets. Peter specifically calls the people to accept Jesus as their Redeemer by designating Jesus as the prophet like Moses. He says,

> For Moses said, "The Lord your God will raise up for you a prophet like me from among your own people. To him you shall listen in whatever he tells you. Everyone who refuses to listen to that prophet will be cut off from the people."
>
> Acts 3:22-23

When the deacon Stephen is on trial before the Sanhedrin, he delivers a scathing accusation of those who reject Jesus. He recites how the children of Israel had rejected Moses. He reminds them that "it was this Moses who said to the children of Israel, 'God will raise up from you, from among your own people, a prophet like me'" (Acts 7:37). They rejected Moses. They now are turning away from Jesus, the prophet like Moses.

St. Cyril of Alexandria once wrote, “All that is written about the blessed Moses we affirm to be an icon and a type of that salvation which comes in Christ” (*Glaphyra on Exodus 1:3*). Most certainly, Moses’ giving the manna in the desert was a type or prefigurement of Jesus’ feeding the five thousand with bread. There is no surprise, therefore, that, in the miracle of the multiplication of loaves and fish, the people recognized Jesus as the New Moses and as someone even greater.

The day after the miracle of the multiplication of loaves and fish, the people went looking for Jesus because they had eaten the bread He gave them and were satisfied (Jn 6:26). They demanded from Jesus some proof that he is truly the Messiah. They say, “What sign can you give us that we can see and come to believe in you? Our ancestors ate manna in the desert. As it is written, ‘he gave them bread from heaven’ to eat” (Jn 6:30-31). In response, Jesus Himself tells them that both the manna in the desert and the bread He gave them were but a foretaste of the Eucharist. He is the true bread from heaven (Jn 6:32-35).

The manna Moses had provided was sufficient for the needs of the day. The bread

Jesus had multiplied was more than the people could possibly eat in one day. But the Eucharist is the Bread of Life. It is Jesus who gives us His very Body and Blood to sustain us through the wilderness of this world. The Eucharist is Jesus who accompanies us on our life journey, supporting us and leading us as the New Moses to the Promised Land.

> *In those days Moses raised his hands to heaven and brought down manna, the bread of angels; the New Moses raises his hands to heaven and gives us the food of eternal life.*
>
> St. John Chrysostom, Cat. 3, 24-27

PRAYERS

O God, come to my assistance.
O Lord, make haste to help me.

Glory be to the Father, and to the Son
And to the Holy Spirit.
As it was in the beginning is now
and ever shall be, world without end. Amen.

Prayer for the Third Day

Father, You appointed Moses to lead Your people out of slavery in Egypt through the wilderness to the Promised Land. With

manna from heaven, You nourished and sustained them on their arduous journey. Through the wilderness of our lives, we now follow Jesus whom You have appointed as Lord and Messiah, "deserving of a greater glory than Moses" (Heb 3:3). He feeds us with the Living Bread of Heaven, giving us His own Body as true food and His Blood as true drink to sustain us on our journey to our heavenly Promised Land. Strengthened by this great gift of the Eucharist, keep us always faithful to Him who is Lord forever and ever. Amen.

Prayer of Adoration

Lord Jesus Christ, I adore and I worship You present in the Blessed Sacrament. I thank You for Your great love in giving us Your very Body and Blood, Soul and Divinity in the Eucharist. I truly believe that You are present in this great Sacrament of the Altar. Night and day, You remain with us, drawing us closer to Your Most Sacred Heart, full of compassion and mercy for us poor sinners. I offer You all my thoughts, words, deeds, and affections. Graciously accept the homage of my life. By the grace of the Holy Spirit, make me love You more and more so that I may love all others in Your

Name and be pleasing to the Father. You who live and reign forever and ever. Amen.

Prayer of Petition

Father Most Merciful, I praise and thank You for the gift of Jesus, Your only begotten Son whom You sent as our Savior and Redeemer. I truly believe that Jesus who remains with us in the Most Blessed Sacrament of the Altar stands before Your throne of grace, making constant intercession for us. In His outstretched hands, I place my fervent prayer (here mention your intentions). Have mercy on me and answer me according to Your holy will. With full confidence in Your kindness, I offer my prayer in the Name of Jesus who lives and reigns with You in the unity of the Holy Spirit, God, forever and ever. Amen.

Prayer to Our Blessed Mother

O Mary, most blessed of all women, to you we come in humble petition. From you, Virgin Immaculate, the Son of God took flesh and became our Savior. By His Suffering, Death, and Resurrection, He has won for us the forgiveness of our sins and the gift of eternal life. Mother of the

Redeemer, look with pity on us and help us grow in a greater and greater devotion to the Eucharist, the very Body and Blood, Soul and Divinity of your beloved Son. Through your powerful intercession, Refuge of sinners, gain for us true sorrow for our sins so that we may worthily share in the Eucharist, the Sacrifice of the Cross made present to us, and, with firm faith, receive Him in Holy Communion. Mother of Divine Grace, assist us with your prayers so that our whole lives become an act of adoration and praise of Jesus who is Lord forever and ever. Amen.

O Sacrament Most Holy,
O Sacrament Divine!
All praise and all thanksgiving
be every moment Thine.

For additional prayers see page 113

Fourth Day 4

The Word of God

"The Word became flesh and dwelt among us."

Jn 1:14

No prophet in the Old Testament resembles Moses more than the ninth century prophet Elijah (1 Ki 17:1–2 Ki 2:12). He abruptly appears on the national scene at a time when Baalism, a pagan fertility cult, was threatening the religion founded by Moses. With dramatic intensity, such as calling down fire from heaven on Mt. Carmel, Elijah worked eight miracles to bring the people back to the covenant Moses had established. He died the way he lived. He was taken up to heaven in a whirlwind and fiery chariot. At God's command, Elijah trained Elisha to succeed him in the prophetic office (1 Ki 19:16).

When Elijah was taken up to heaven in a fiery chariot, his mantle fell to Elisha and God granted him a double portion of Elijah's spirit (2 Ki 2:9-14). Like Elijah, he worked miracles. As Elijah had brought back to life

the son of the widow of Zarephath (1 Ki 17: 17-24), Elisha resurrected the son of the woman of Shunem (2 Ki 4:18-37).

In both instances, the resurrection comes after the women had provided hospitality and food for the prophet. Thus, rabbinic tradition interprets the great virtue of giving food to others as meriting the resurrection of the dead (Cant. Rabbah, 2:5:3). In his graphic portrayal of the final judgment at the end of time, Jesus Himself promises that whoever has given food to the hungry will receive the eternal life won by His Resurrection (Mt 25:34-35).

Elisha was different than his mentor. Elisha was less spectacular but more humane. Responding to everyday human problems, he worked twice as many miracles as Elijah. He is a type of Jesus.

In responding to the Jews' question about Elijah's return before the coming of the Messiah, Jesus points to John the Baptist. John fulfills that expectation. Like Elijah, filled with a holy zeal, the Baptist thunders God's wrath for the unrepentant. As Elisha comes after Elijah, Jesus comes after the Baptist. Like Elisha, Jesus offers hope and healing by working many miracles for ordi-

nary people. And, just as Elisha, so unlike the solitary Elijah, was always in the company of other prophets, so too Jesus accomplished His ministry amidst the crowds and in the company of His apostles. John is the Elijah figure; Jesus, the Elisha figure.

In fact, more than Elijah and even more than Moses himself, Elisha is the Old Testament type foreshadowing the compassionate ministry of Jesus among the people. His miracle of multiplying bread prefigures Jesus' miracle of the multiplication of loaves and fish.

> A man came from Baal-shalishah, and he brought the man of God twenty barley loaves from the first-fruits along with some heads of grain. [Elisha] said, "Give it to the people so that they might eat." His servant said, "What? Should I place this before one hundred men?" But [Elisha] said again, "Give it to the people to eat, for thus says the Lord: They will eat, and there will be some left over." He set it before them, and they ate, and there was some left over, just as the Lord had predicted.
>
> 2 Ki 4:42-44

Elisha headed a school where he taught the Word of God to other prophets. One day during a famine a man from Baal-shalishah brings Elisha twenty loaves of barley bread. It was spring, the time of the first harvest. It was a time of celebration (Lev 23:9-14). Farmers would gather the firstfruits of the land. Those close to Jerusalem would take their offerings to the priests. Those far from the sacred city would bring their gifts to local synagogues and to the prophets among them. In the Old Testament, a gift of food was welcomed at any time; but, at this time, with a dearth of food in the land, this gift was most welcome. Elisha had one hundred prophets to feed.

The anonymous benefactor comes from Baal-Shalishah. The very name of this town includes the name of the pagan fertility god Baal to whom the people are praying for rain. He cannot provide for the basic needs of those who worship him. There is a famine. As then, so today. Whenever we turn to false idols, we suffer. Today a spiritual famine stalks our land. The idols of the world, all those things that we seek to make us happy apart from God, cannot satisfy our most basic needs. Only God can.

When the man from Baal-Shalishah gives Elisha twenty loaves of bread, Elisha instructs his servant to give the bread to the prophets for their meal. Hoarding was not an option. Elisha miraculously provides food for those hundred prophets seeking to know God's Word. This foreshadows Jesus who provides food for those who crowd around Him, seeking to hear God's Word. For God never abandons those who seek His Word. And, in the Eucharist, He offers us that very Word Incarnate.

Elisha multiplies twenty loaves of barley bread baked from the first ripe grain. Bread of the firstfruits. This detail tells us that the event is taking place in the time of the harvest, a time when the people feel the famine most severely. In fact, the fourfold repetition of the verb to eat in just two verses of the text makes us pay attention to the hunger in the empty stomachs of the company of prophets.

In the multiplication of loaves and fish, Jesus Himself pays attention to the empty stomachs of those who have spent hours listening to Him. Even as the large crowd of people are approaching Him, Jesus sees them and already instigates the miracle. He

asks Philip, "Where can we buy bread for them to eat? He said this to test him, because Jesus himself knew what he was going to do" (Jn 6:5-6).

Jesus is ever ready to meet our needs. He hastens to help us in ways unexpected. Even before we come to Him, He is already intent on providing for our needs just as He was for the crowds approaching Him in the deserted place.

In the Eucharist, Jesus is present, abiding and staying with us, longing to satisfy our desire for life itself. We should never waste any time not coming to the Lord. He is constantly making intercession before the Father so that we have all our needs fulfilled, even before we ourselves recognize our needs.

Elisha's miracle of multiplying bread and Jesus' miracle are very similar in the details. However, it is these very details that show the superiority of Jesus. Elisha works the miracle with twenty loaves of barley. He feeds one hundred men. Jesus starts with less, with five loaves, and He feeds the thousands.

Elisha works the miracle by announcing "Thus says the Lord." Notice: it is not

his word, not his command that provides the food. It is God's word. Jesus, however, multiplies bread by His own command. To the prophets of old, the word of God came at moments of revelation and crisis. Jesus is the Word of God made flesh. And He remains with us at all times in the Eucharist.

> *"Rightly then, do we believe that the bread consecrated by the word of God has been made over into the Body of God the Word. For that Body was, as to its potency, bread; but it has been consecrated by the lodging there of the Word, who pitched His tent in the flesh.... It is made over immediately into the Body by means of the word, just as was stated by the Word, "This is My Body!"*
>
> St. Gregory of Nyssa,
> *The Great Catechism*, 37

PRAYERS

O God, come to my assistance.
O Lord, make haste to help me.

Glory be to the Father, and to the Son
And to the Holy Spirit.
As it was in the beginning is now
and ever shall be, world without end. Amen.

Prayer for the Fourth Day

Father, source of all life and holiness, in whose Word the prophet Elisha trusted and thus miraculously fed the hundred prophets with twenty loaves of bread, look with mercy on me. Grant me, I pray, a spirit of trust in Jesus, Your Word Incarnate who Himself is the Bread of life. Give me the confidence to approach the Eucharist with the sure and certain hope of receiving all that I need for my life in this world and for my eternal salvation. Inspire me to care, as Jesus did, for the welfare of others. Gently lead me by the Holy Spirit to always turn to Jesus so as to find in Him the grace to do Your holy will. Who live and reign forever and ever. Amen.

Prayer of Adoration

Lord Jesus Christ, I adore and I worship You present in the Blessed Sacrament. I thank You for Your great love in giving us Your very Body and Blood, Soul and Divinity in the Eucharist. I truly believe that You are present in this great Sacrament of the Altar. Night and day, You remain with us, drawing us closer to Your Most Sacred Heart, full of compassion and mercy for us poor sinners. I offer You all my thoughts,

words, deeds, and affections. Graciously accept the homage of my life. By the grace of the Holy Spirit, make me love You more and more so that I may love all others in Your Name and be pleasing to the Father. You who live and reign forever and ever. Amen.

Prayer of Petition

Father Most Merciful, I praise and thank You for the gift of Jesus, Your only begotten Son whom You sent as our Savior and Redeemer. I truly believe that Jesus who remains with us in the Most Blessed Sacrament of the Altar stands before Your throne of grace, making constant intercession for us. In His outstretched hands, I place my fervent prayer (*here mention your intentions*). Have mercy on me and answer me according to Your holy will. With full confidence in Your kindness, I offer my prayer in the Name of Jesus who lives and reigns with You in the unity of the Holy Spirit, God, forever and ever. Amen.

Prayer to Our Blessed Mother

O Mary, most blessed of all women, to you we come in humble petition. From you, Virgin Immaculate, the Son of God took flesh

and became our Savior. By His Suffering, Death, and Resurrection, He has won for us the forgiveness of our sins and the gift of eternal life. Mother of the Redeemer, look with pity on us and help us grow in a greater and greater devotion to the Eucharist, the very Body and Blood, Soul and Divinity of your beloved Son. Through your powerful intercession, Refuge of sinners, gain for us true sorrow for our sins so that we may worthily share in the Eucharist, the Sacrifice of the Cross made present to us, and, with firm faith, receive Him in Holy Communion. Mother of Divine Grace, assist us with your prayers so that our whole lives become an act of adoration and praise of Jesus who is Lord forever and ever. Amen.

O Sacrament Most Holy,
O Sacrament Divine!
All praise and all thanksgiving
be every moment Thine.

For additional prayers see page 113

Fifth Day 5

The Banquet of Wisdom

"Christ is the power of God and the wisdom of God."
1 Cor 1:24

A good story abounds with details. Its author engages the reader with specifics, not generalizations. Details matter. For example, the Dutch philosopher Erasmus once wrote, "When I get a little money, I buy books. If any is left, I buy food and clothes." His words are concrete. The details he lists make all the difference in effectively communicating his thought in a memorable way. In biblical narratives, the details are not simply embellishments on the text.

All the gospels remember that Jesus works the miracle with just five loaves of bread and two fish. In the fourth gospel, Andrew says, "There is a boy here who has five barley loaves and two fish. But what help will they be among so many?" (Jn 6:9). The evangelist mentions two details that the other gospels pass over. He tells us that the loaves were barley bread and that they came from the hands of a young boy. These small details open for us great insights into the miracle.

John designates the young boy with the Greek word παιδάριον (paidarion). This word is a double diminutive in Greek. It means not just boy but a little boy. It can also mean servant. This word appears nowhere else in the New Testament. But it does appear in the Greek Old Testament to designate Elisha's servant (2 Ki 4:38; 2 Ki 4:43). The word "barley"(κρίθινος: *krithinos*) appears in the story of Elisha's miracle of multiplying bread and nowhere else in the New Testament except in John's account of Jesus' multiplication of loaves and fish (Jn 6:9-13).

Most certainly John includes these details about the little boy and the barley to make us recall the miracle of Elisha who multiplied bread to feed the hundred prophets in a time of famine (2 Ki 4:42-44). Jesus is repeating the same miracle that Elisha did, but now with greater power. The bread He provides is not reserved, as in the miracle of Elisha, for prophets who dedicate their lives to the Word of God, but is generously given to the crowds hungry for God's Word.

Jesus has come to open the limits of God's care. As Paul reminds us, "Jesus came…to [those] who were far away and….to those

who were near. For through him, we both have access to the Father in the one Spirit" (Eph 2:17-18). We are now "members of the household of God" (Eph 2:19), called to share at the one table of the Bread of Life.

But John would have us see something even more profound in the multiplication of loaves and fish. In his gospel, John views Jesus through the lens of the Wisdom tradition of the Old Testament. For example, in the prologue to his gospel (Jn 1:1-18), John strongly echoes the Wisdom language of Judaism during the Second Temple period.

The Word pre-exists before the creation of the world (Jn 1:1-2), just as Wisdom exists before God begins to create (Prov 8:22-31; Sir 24:3-6). And, just as Wisdom comes to dwell on earth, pitching her tent and dwells among God's people (Sir 24:8), "The Word became flesh and dwelt (ἐσκήνωσεν: *eskēnōsen*, i.e. to pitch one's tent or to dwell) among us" (Jn 1:14). Jesus, the Divine Logos, the Word preexisting from all eternity in the bosom of the Father, is Wisdom Incarnate.

In ancient Greece, people had the custom of gathering for a banquet (symposium) where they shared not only food and drink but also wisdom as well. In the Wisdom tra-

dition of the Old Testament, Wisdom herself prepares such a banquet. She invites all to come.

> Wisdom has built her house; she has hewn her seven pillars. She has slain her animals and mixed her wine, and she has spread her table. She has sent forth her maidservants and proclaimed from the heights of the city, "Let all those who are simple turn in here." To the person without understanding she says, "Come and partake of my food and taste the wine that I have prepared! Abandon foolishness so that you may live; walk in the way of understanding."
>
> Prov 9:1-6

Wisdom is a generous hostess. Unlike the host of a Greek symposium, she invites everyone. Not just the elite, the wealthy or the wise, but the ordinary, the laborer, and the child are invited. At her banquet, the simple and unlearned become wise.

In John's gospel, after multiplying the bread and fish, Jesus promises that one day He was going to give His Body and Blood as our food and drink. He Himself is the Bread of Life. He is Wisdom Incarnate who offers

the banquet for all to feast on. Everyone is invited. Jesus' miracle of the multiplication of bread already points to His greater gift of the Eucharist.

Like the evangelist John, the early Christians both in their hymns and creeds identified Jesus as the Wisdom of God (St. Athanasius, *Oratio* 2, 78. 81-82). They understood that, as Wisdom Incarnate, Jesus calls all to share in the banquet He prepares in the Eucharist. The Eucharist is the banquet of Divine Wisdom.

In the Eucharist, we receive into our heart and soul Jesus, the Wisdom of God Incarnate. He comes to instruct us and guide us. He gives us the strength to "abandon foolishness...and... to walk in the way of understanding" (Prov 9:6). Feasting at Wisdom's banquet, we receive what is more precious than all this world's wealth. We receive the gift of life. Wisdom once said in the Old Testament, "For by me your days will be multiplied, and years will be added to your life" (Prov 9:11). Jesus, Wisdom Incarnate, says to us who eat the Bread of Life, "Whoever feeds upon my flesh and drinks my blood has eternal life" (Jn 6:54).

"'And she [Wisdom] has furnished her table' [Prov. 9:2] . . . refers to [Christ's] honored and undefiled body and blood, which day by day are administered and offered sacrificially at the spiritual divine table, as a memorial of that first and ever-memorable table of the spiritual divine supper."

St. Hippolytus, *Fragment from Commentary on Proverbs*

PRAYERS

O God, come to my assistance.
O Lord, make haste to help me.

Glory be to the Father, and to the Son
And to the Holy Spirit.
As it was in the beginning is now
and ever shall be, world without end. Amen.

Prayer for the Fifth Day

Eternal and Incarnate Wisdom, most lovable and adorable Jesus, true God and true man, only Son of the eternal Father and of Mary always Virgin, I adore You profoundly, dwelling in the splendor of Your Father from all eternity, and in the virginal womb of Mary, Your most worthy Mother, at the

time of Your Incarnation. I thank You for having emptied Yourself in assuming the condition of a slave to set me free from the cruel slavery of the evil one…

I confess with my mouth that You, Jesus, are Lord, the Ruler over all. You are the Christ, the Son of God. I believe in my heart that God raised You from the dead and You are alive forevermore, seated on Your throne in heaven next to the Father. The heavenly hosts worship before Your throne. I believe Your blood that was shed on the cross washes away all my sins…I give myself wholly to [You] Jesus Christ, the Incarnate Wisdom.

St. Louis Marie Grignion de Montfort

Prayer of Adoration

Lord Jesus Christ, I adore and I worship You present in the Blessed Sacrament. I thank You for Your great love in giving us Your very Body and Blood, Soul and Divinity in the Eucharist. I truly believe that You are present in this great Sacrament of the Altar. Night and day, You remain with us, drawing us closer to Your Most Sacred Heart, full of compassion and mercy for us poor sinners. I offer You all my thoughts, words, deeds, and affections. Graciously

accept the homage of my life. By the grace of the Holy Spirit, make me love You more and more so that I may love all others in Your Name and be pleasing to the Father. You who live and reign forever and ever. Amen

Prayer of Petition

Father Most Merciful, I praise and thank You for the gift of Jesus, Your only begotten Son whom You sent as our Savior and Redeemer. I truly believe that Jesus who remains with us in the Most Blessed Sacrament of the Altar stands before Your throne of grace, making constant intercession for us. In His outstretched hands, I place my fervent prayer (*here mention your intentions*). Have mercy on me and answer me according to Your holy will. With full confidence in Your kindness, I offer my prayer in the Name of Jesus who lives and reigns with You in the unity of the Holy Spirit, God, forever and ever. Amen.

Prayer to Our Blessed Mother

O Mary, most blessed of all women, to you we come in humble petition. From you, Virgin Immaculate, the Son of God took flesh and became our Savior. By His Suffering,

Death and Resurrection, He has won for us the forgiveness of our sins and the gift of eternal life. Mother of the Redeemer, look with pity on us and help us grow in a greater and greater devotion to the Eucharist, the very Body and Blood, Soul and Divinity of your beloved Son. Through your powerful intercession, Refuge of sinners, gain for us true sorrow for our sins so that we may worthily share in the Eucharist, the Sacrifice of the Cross made present to us, and, with firm faith, receive Him in Holy Communion. Mother of Divine Grace, assist us with your prayers so that our whole lives become an act of adoration and praise of Jesus who is Lord forever and ever. Amen.

O Sacrament Most Holy,
O Sacrament Divine!
All praise and all thanksgiving
be every moment Thine.

For additional prayers see page 113

Sixth Day

The Hands of Jesus

6

"Do not fear, for I am with you; do not be afraid, for I am your God. I will strengthen you and give you help. I will uphold you with my victorious right hand."
Isa 41:10

Before Saul ascended the throne as the first king of Israel, God's people were ruled by a succession of twelve charismatic leaders called judges. These popular heroes were individuals chosen by God to meet an imminent crisis and then return to their normal way of life. Shamgar, a simple farmer, was the third of these judges. He is easily overlooked since he appears in only one verse in the Bible and then disappears. "Shamgar, the son of Anath...killed six hundred Philistines with an oxgoad, and he delivered Israel" (Jdg 3:31). The small detail of his weapon is immensely significant.

An oxgoad was a sturdy stick measuring almost ten feet long six inches in diameter. At one end, there was attached a metal tip to prod the oxen to keep plowing. On the other end, there was a curved blade for cleaning out the plow. With this very unremarkable

farm tool, this heroic farmer wipes out six hundred trained soldiers of Israel's enemy. An incredible victory! The mention of the oxgoad may seem at first an unimportant detail. But it impresses on our minds with great impact the fact that Shamgar's success belongs totally to God.

With a similar intent, God sets the cowardly Gideon over a small army of three hundred soldiers. Holding flares and making noise with their pitchers, they destroy the well-armed Midianites outnumbering them four hundred and fifty to one (Jdg 7:16-22). Similarly God puts the jawbone of an ass in the hands of Samson and he slays a thousand Philistines (Jdg 15:15-16). God also places a slingshot in the nimble hands of the young David; and, Goliath is destroyed (1 Sam 17:50). In each case, it is not the skill or strength of the individual or the means he uses, but it is the divine power of God who, with the most insignificant means, accomplishes great things beyond human capacity.

So it is in the miracle of the multiplication of the loaves and fish. With more than five thousand tired and hungry men, women, and children, God places in the hands of Jesus five barley loaves and two fish. Certainly not

enough to feed even one person! And not the best of fare either. Yet all eat and are satisfied.

The fourth evangelist tells us that the two fish were little fish. He uses the diminutive Greek word ὀψάρια (*opsaria*: small fish). This word is only found in John's gospel. It refers to small fish no bigger than sardines. The Sea of Galilee was abundantly rich with these fish. The fishermen in the area would dry and salt them or pickle them. They would sell these fish to be used as a relish when eaten with bread. These inexpensive fish were not much of a meal by themselves.

The bread placed in Jesus' hands was made from barley. Barley cost only a third of the price of wheat. It was a coarse bread that the ancients demeaned. Plutarch graphically describes the abject conditions to which the Persian king Artaxerxes Mnemon was reduced by saying he had to eat barley bread. Livy relates how soldiers who had lost their standards were punished by being given barley for food. And, according to Suetonius, Caelius in order to show his utter disdain for a certain public speaker labels him a barley-bread orator.

In biblical tradition, wheat was for man; barley, for animals (1 Ki 4:28). Thus, to con-

demn the greed of false prophetesses who prophesy for the meanest recompense, God says, "You have dishonored me in the eyes of my people for a few handfuls of barley and a few scraps of bread" (Ezek 13:19).

Five barely loaves and two dried fish, the most inexpensive and lowly sustenance, are placed in the hands of Jesus. These are not ordinary hands, but the human hands of the master craftsman who fashioned creation. These are the hands of the Word Incarnate "through [whom] all things came into existence" (Jn 1:3). With his prayer of blessing, the most insignificant of elements become a banquet for thousands. Already Jesus is foreshadowing the Last Supper when His word will change ordinary bread and common wine into His Body and Blood, the richest banquet the world has ever known.

At times, we may feel totally insufficient to make a difference in our world. We are weak, but God is strong. When we place ourselves in the hands of Jesus, our weakness matters not. St. Paul reminds us of this.

> Not many of you were wise by human standards, not many were powerful, not many were of noble birth. Rather God chose those who were regarded as

foolish by the world to shame the wise; God chose those in the world who were weak to shame the strong, God chose those in the world who were lowly and despised, those who count for nothing, to reduce to nothing those who were regarded as worthy, so that no one could boast in the presence of God. It is through him that you are in Christ Jesus, who became for us wisdom of God, as well as righteousness, sanctification, and redemption.

1 Cor 1:26-30

Through the precious gift of the Eucharist, we who receive the Body of Christ become the Body of Christ for the world. Touched with His omnipotence, we become the means to satisfy the world's deepest hunger for truth and goodness. Now that Jesus has ascended to heaven, He has more rather than less power. He can use us with all our weaknesses and inabilities to accomplish His own glorious purposes. We need never lose heart.

Behold the mystery of your salvation
laid out for you;
behold what you are, become what you
receive.

St. Augustine, *Sermon 57*, On the Holy Eucharist

PRAYERS

O God, come to my assistance.
O Lord, make haste to help me.

Glory be to the Father, and to the Son
And to the Holy Spirit.
As it was in the beginning is now
and ever shall be, world without end. Amen.

Prayer for the Sixth Day

Lord Jesus Christ, You do not disdain the poor and lowly. Look kindly on my ignorance, my weakness and want of talent. Apart from You, I can do nothing. In Your generous hands, five barley loaves became a feast for thousands. Into those hands, now bearing the nail prints of the Cross, I place my entire self. I give you my life and all I possess, begging You to use me according to Your holy will so that others may come to know the abundance of Your love and mercy. You who live and reign with the Father and the Holy Spirit, God, forever and ever. Amen.

Prayer of Adoration

Lord Jesus Christ, I adore and I worship You present in the Blessed Sacrament. I thank You for Your great love in giving us Your very Body and Blood, Soul and

Divinity in the Eucharist. I truly believe that You are present in this great Sacrament of the Altar. Night and day, You remain with us, drawing us closer to Your Most Sacred Heart, full of compassion and mercy for us poor sinners. I offer You all my thoughts, words, deeds, and affections. Graciously accept the homage of my life. By the grace of the Holy Spirit, make me love You more and more so that I may love all others in Your Name and be pleasing to the Father. You who live and reign forever and ever. Amen.

Prayer of Petition

Father Most Merciful, I praise and thank you for the gift of Jesus, Your only begotten Son whom You sent as our Savior and Redeemer. I truly believe that Jesus who remains with us in the Most Blessed Sacrament of the Altar stands before Your throne of grace, making constant intercession for us. In His outstretched hands, I place my fervent prayer (*here mention your intentions*). Have mercy on me and answer me according to Your holy will. With full confidence in Your kindness, I offer my prayer in the Name of Jesus who lives and reigns with You in the unity of the Holy Spirit, God, forever and ever. Amen.

Prayer to Our Blessed Mother

O Mary, most blessed of all women, to you we come in humble petition. From you, Virgin Immaculate, the Son of God took flesh and became our Savior. By His Suffering, Death, and Resurrection, He has won for us the forgiveness of our sins and the gift of eternal life. Mother of the Redeemer, look with pity on us and help us grow in a greater devotion to the Eucharist, the very Body and Blood, Soul and Divinity of your beloved Son. Through your powerful intercession, Refuge of sinners, gain for us true sorrow for our sins so that we may worthily share in the Eucharist, the Sacrifice of the Cross made present to us, and, with firm faith, receive Him in Holy Communion. Mother of Divine Grace, assist us with your prayers so that our whole lives become an act of adoration and praise of Jesus who is Lord forever and ever. Amen.

O Sacrament Most Holy,
O Sacrament Divine!
All praise and all thanksgiving
be every moment Thine.

For additional prayers see page 113

Seventh Day

7

The Pledge of Future Glory

"Whoever feeds upon my flesh and drinks my blood has eternal life. And I will raise him up on the last day."

Jn 6:54

Coincidences happen. A chance meeting with an old friend. Being at the right place at the right time. Saying the appropriate word to someone without even realizing it. Swiss psychiatrist Carl Jung created the label "synchronicity" to analyze these meaningful happenings that seem to have no apparent causal connection. However, French novelist Anatole France, the 1921 Nobel Prize Winner in Literature, astutely remarked that coincidence and chance are simply pseudonyms for God when He does not leave His signature on an event or happening. Even Albert Einstein is allegedly credited with saying, "Coincidence is God's way of remaining anonymous."

In the miracle of the multiplication of loaves and fish, it seems as if it is by mere coincidence that there is a little boy with his loaves and fish. All the evangelists mention the number of loaves and fish, but only John

tells us that these come from the hands of a little boy (Jn 6:9). The other evangelists take no notice of him. For them, the loaves and fish are more important.

There were many children among the crowd that day with their families (Mt 14:21). Jesus always welcomed children. He even rebuked His disciples when they tried to keep them away from Him (Mt 19:13-15: Lk 18:15-17). But it is no mere coincidence that this particular young boy is where the apostles can spot the five loaves and two fish in his basket.

God's providence guides and rules over all. Providence is simply God governing creation as a loving Father and working all things for the good He intends. God places this lad before the eyes of the apostles. God can work even through the children among us. Age is no limit to serving the Lord.

We do not know the name of the lad with the five loaves and two fish and we can only surmise why he was present at this great event. On the one hand, he is near enough to the apostles for Andrew to notice him. The Greek word for young boy (παιδάριον: *paidarion*) could mean "servant" or "helper" as it does in the Old Testament story of

Elisha. Perhaps the young boy is accompanying the apostles and carrying their meager provisions for their travels.

On the other hand, Philip's words about buying food may imply that this little boy was selling bread and fish for the people to snack on. He knew where the crowd was going to spend some time and he was enterprising enough to find a way to make a profit. Whether accompanying the apostles or coming on his own, divine providence positions him in a prominent place to be seen. God is never without the means to care for those in need, whether their need is physical or spiritual.

We can be sure that the apostles did not constrain the young boy to hand over his loaves and fish. Rather, he takes what is his and gives it freely to them. Not selfishly holding on to what he has yet to sell, he willingly parts with it. His offering placed in the hands of Jesus becomes a great feast. The thousands eat and are satisfied. And, more than that, this generous lad shares in the abundance of all that was left over. Christ empties our hands only to fill them with more than we can imagine. Anything we place in the hands of Jesus is well invested.

All the gifts that God gives us are not for us alone. We are to use our gifts to help others. Talent, expertise, money, knowledge, time, position, and influence are some of the blessings we receive. King David knew this. Before he closed his eyes in death, he stood before the people and publicly acknowledged that all the wealth and power that had come into his hands were gifts from the generous hands of God. He extolled God saying, “Now, our God, we thank you, and we praise your glorious name…All things belong to you, and everything that we have given you is from your hand” (1 Chr 29:13-14). A grateful heart recognizes God’s hand in all things. The secret of joy is this: “In all created things discern the providence and wisdom of God, and in all things give Him thanks” (St. Teresa of Avila).

Everything we have is on loan from God. There is nothing that belongs to us absolutely. God’s gifts are a sacred trust. We cannot foolishly claim that we own what we have. We are merely given all we have to be used for our own good and the good of others. Even our very life is on loan from God. That is why Jesus tell us that one day God will demand it back (Lk 12:20). However, when we generously place what we have in the

hands of Jesus, we, like the lad in the miracle, are left amazed at what Christ can do with what we have returned to Him.

The timing of the miracle of the loaves and fish is freighted with meaning. It is the time of the Passover. The barley is ripe for harvest. According to God's command (Lev 23:9-14), the people were to bring the first gleanings of the barley, "the firstfruits," to the Temple in Jerusalem. The Law stipulated that an omer of barley should be offered to God. That would be the amount of barley needed to make five loaves of bread. Thus, when the young boy offers Jesus his five loaves made from the new barley recently harvested, he is literally making a sacrifice to God, because Jesus is truly God.

Furthermore, the offering of "the firstfruits" of the barley at Passover time commemorated God's choice of Israel as His own firstborn in the Exodus (Ex 4:22). Separated from the nations, Israel was the firstfruits of redemption, the beginning of an abundant harvest. When offering the barley, the priest lifted up the sheaf and "waved" it before the Lord (Lev 23:11-12). How strikingly symbolic! The seed that had died and was buried in the ground rose to new life and

now was lifted up and brought into God's presence. In this is foreshadowed Christ's Resurrection which took place at the very time of the barley offering.

Christ died and was buried and rose from the dead. He has been lifted up into the presence of God in his heavenly Temple. As Paul says, He is the firstfruits of God's harvest of those redeemed by the blood of Christ. Christ's Resurrection is not the end of God's work. It is the beginning of bringing to completion the day when God will be all in all.

> Christ has been raised from the dead, the firstfruits of those who have fallen asleep. For since death came into the world through a man, the resurrection of the dead has also come through a man. Just as in Adam all die, so all will be brought to life in Christ, but each one in proper order: Christ, the firstfruits; afterward, at his coming, those who belong to Christ. Then comes the end when he hands over the kingdom to God the Father… so that God may be all in all.
>
> 1 Cor 15:20-24, 28

As the firstfruits were gathered on the day after the Sabbath, Jesus, the firstfruits of the

dead, rose on the day after the Sabbath. As the firstfruits offered to God were a sacrifice of thanksgiving which sanctified the harvest, the Risen Jesus is our thanksgiving, our Eucharist. In receiving Him, in feasting on His Body and Blood, we are sanctified and given the pledge and promise of our own resurrection. Thus, in every desert of life where we wander, in loneliness, grief, misunderstanding and sickness, the Eucharist is our hope and joy. The Eucharist is the pledge of our future glory.

> *In instituting the sacrament of the Eucharist, Jesus anticipates and makes present the sacrifice of the Cross and the victory of the resurrection.*
>
> Pope Benedict XVI,
> *Sacramentum Caritatis*, 10

PRAYERS

O God, come to my assistance.
O Lord, make haste to help me.

Glory be to the Father, and to the Son
And to the Holy Spirit.
As it was in the beginning is now
and ever shall be, world without end. Amen.

Prayer for the Seventh Day

Father Most Holy, in Your ineffable providence, You glorified Your Son by raising Him from the dead and sending us the Holy Spirit to guide and direct us on our earthly pilgrimage. By the power of the Holy Spirit, Your Church offers us the Bread of life to strengthen us and even now make us partakers of Your divine life. May our sharing in the Gift of the Body and Blood of Your only begotten Son make our faith stronger, our hope surer and our charity purer. Grant, we pray, that the Eucharist open for us the way to eternal life. Through Christ our Lord. Amen.

Prayer of Adoration

Lord Jesus Christ, I adore and I worship You present in the Blessed Sacrament. I thank You for Your great love in giving us Your very Body and Blood, Soul and Divinity in the Eucharist. I truly believe that You are present in this great Sacrament of the Altar. Night and day, You remain with us, drawing us closer to Your Most Sacred Heart, full of compassion and mercy for us poor sinners. I offer You all my thoughts, words, deeds, and affections. Graciously

accept the homage of my life. By the grace of the Holy Spirit, make me love You more and more so that I may love all others in Your Name and be pleasing to the Father. You who live and reign forever and ever. Amen.

Prayer of Petition

Father Most Merciful, I praise and thank You for the gift of Jesus, Your only begotten Son whom You sent as our Savior and Redeemer. I truly believe that Jesus who remains with us in the Most Blessed Sacrament of the Altar stands before Your throne of grace, making constant intercession for us. In His outstretched hands, I place my fervent prayer (*here mention your intentions*). Have mercy on me and answer me according to Your holy will. With full confidence in Your kindness, I offer my prayer in the Name of Jesus who lives and reigns with You in the unity of the Holy Spirit, God, forever and ever. Amen.

Prayer to Our Blessed Mother

O Mary, most blessed of all women, to you we come in humble petition. From you, Virgin Immaculate, the Son of God took flesh and became our Savior. By His

Suffering, Death, and Resurrection, He has won for us the forgiveness of our sins and the gift of eternal life. Mother of the Redeemer, look with pity on us and help us grow in a greater and greater devotion to the Eucharist, the very Body and Blood, Soul and Divinity of your beloved Son. Through your powerful intercession, Refuge of sinners, gain for us true sorrow for our sins so that we may worthily share in the Eucharist, the Sacrifice of the Cross made present to us, and, with firm faith, receive Him in Holy Communion. Mother of Divine Grace, assist us with your prayers so that our whole lives become an act of adoration and praise of Jesus who is Lord forever and ever. Amen.

O Sacrament Most Holy,
O Sacrament Divine!
All praise and all thanksgiving
be every moment Thine.

For additional prayers see page 113

Eighth Day

Bread Broken for Others

8

"You give them something to eat yourselves."

Mt 14:16

Bethsaida is third only to Jerusalem and Capernaum in the number of times mentioned in the New Testament. It was one of the three towns where Jesus worked many of His miracles (Mt 11:20-21). Bethsaida ('House of Fish') was located on the eastern shore of the Sea of Galilee. Its hard-working people made their living by fishing and by serving the merchants on the road from the Mediterranean coast to Syria. Near to this city, there were deserts of extensive uninhabited lands. Luke tells us that, in one such lonely place, Jesus worked the miracle of the multiplication of loaves and fish.

The crowds had flocked to hear Jesus and to be healed. When the hour grew late, the apostles grew impatient. They had come to this place to be alone with Jesus. The work day was almost over. It was about three in the afternoon and they want Jesus to send the people into the surrounding villages to

buy food and find shelter for the night (Lk 9:12). In this, the apostles show their concern for the temporal needs of the people and set an example for all who would follow Jesus. We are called to care for the physical well-being of one another, not just each other's spiritual welfare.

Jesus refuses to dismiss the crowds. He "knew what he was going to do" (Jn 6:6). He tests Philip. Philip was a down-to-earth person, keen on seeing the tangible (Jn 14:8). When Nathaniel objected to Philip's invitation to meet Jesus, Philip simply answered, "Come and see" (Jn 1:46).

At the Last Supper, Jesus said, "If you know me, then you will know my Father also. From now on you do know him. You have seen him" (Jn 14:7). Philip interrupted Jesus and said, "Lord, show us the Father, and it will be enough for us" (Jn 14:8). Philip was a matter-of-fact individual, dependent on his own ability to size up a situation. He was quick to ask for proof for what Jesus said.

Jesus wants to widen Philip's view of reality. He asks Philip, "Where are we to buy bread for them to eat?" (Jn 6:5). Philip was from Bethsaida. He would most certainly know where to go. They were in a desert

place and he knew that there were no stores nearby. He also knew that the apostles had little money in their common purse.

Philip shrewdly calculates their resources. He immediately responds to Jesus' question. He boldly announces, "Two hundred days' wages would not buy enough bread for each of them to have a small piece" (Jn 6:7). He sees no possible way to feed the people. He is myopic. He limits his vision to what he and the other apostles can manage. He does not take into account what Jesus can do.

Deliberately Jesus has put Philip in a situation where he sees no human solution and where he does not even think of a divine solution. With Jesus present, we are never limited by our abilities and resources. Jesus wants us, like Philip, to realize that, in every human predicament, He is ready to assist us with His divine help. The miracle Jesus is about to work will indelibly etch this truth on Philip's mind.

While Philip calculates the demand, Andrew turns his eye to the supply. He spots a young boy with five loaves and two small fish. He immediately brings the boy to Jesus. Every time Andrew stands out in the gospel, he is introducing someone to Jesus.

At the beginning of Jesus' ministry, Andrew brings his brother Peter to Jesus (Jn 1:40-42). During the final days of Jesus' life, he introduces the Greeks to Him (Jn 12:20-22). And, in the middle of Jesus' public life, he brings the boy with the five loaves and two fish to Jesus (Jn 6:8-9).

Andrew was always eager to share Jesus with others. Not only was he the first disciple of Jesus, he was the first missionary. He did not keep Jesus to himself. He understood that there was no one Jesus would not like to see. How blessed we would be if more of us had the same missionary heart as Andrew!

Andrew introduces the young boy to Jesus, saying, "There is a boy here who has five barley loaves and two fish. But what help will they be among so many" (Jn 6:9). He sees the situation as hopeless as does Philip. Both apostles had been with Jesus from the beginning. But the miracle of Cana has already faded from their memory. They see only the human need. They have yet to learn the greatness of Jesus who cares for every aspect of our lives. As Fulton Sheen once so wisely said, "In the reckoning of men there is always a deficit; in the arithmetic of God, there is always a surplus."

Neither Philip nor Andrew knew what to do. But Jesus did! He was equal to the situation. No one went away without sharing in His goodness. What His own apostles judged insufficient was more than sufficient for what Jesus intended to do. Satan will always turn our attention to ourselves and to the paltry means at our disposal to do good for others. He thrills to see us fret in despair and recoil from meeting the needs of the poor, the hungry, the marginalized, and the rejected.

However, Jesus who multiplies bread and fish with His divine power calmed the sea and trampled death beneath His feet. He reigns as Lord. Heaven is His throne and nature, His servant. He now stands before us with all His power as God in the Eucharist. We can confidently approach Him. Once we fix our eyes on Jesus, despair vanishes like a cloud before the blazing sun and our soul is filled with hope, "For nothing will be impossible for God" (Lk 1:37).

> *The Eucharist…compels all who believe in him to become "bread that is broken" for others, and to work for the building of a more just and fraternal world. Keeping in mind the multiplication of the loaves and fishes,*

we need to realize that Christ continues today to exhort his disciples to become personally engaged: "You yourselves, give them something to eat" (Mt 14:16). Each of us is truly called, together with Jesus, to be bread broken for the life of the world.

Pope Benedict XVI,
Sacramentum Caritatis, 88

PRAYERS

O God, come to my assistance.
O Lord, make haste to help me.

Glory be to the Father, and to the Son
And to the Holy Spirit.
As it was in the beginning is now
and ever shall be, world without end. Amen.

Prayer for the Eighth Day

Lord Jesus Christ, look kindly upon the many people today who suffer hunger and want, both spiritual and material. Grant us who venerate and adore You in the Eucharist to be worthy members of Your Body the Church. Make us hunger and thirst for justice for all our brothers and sisters throughout the world. With the light of Your truth, open our eyes to the sufferings

of those who long for justice. With Your steadfast goodness, open our hands that we may generously share the gifts You give us. In Your mercy, Lord, fill our hearts with the fire of Your Holy Spirit that we may love all others as You love us. You who live and reign with the Father and the Holy Spirit, God, forever and ever. Amen.

Prayer of Adoration

Lord Jesus Christ, I adore and I worship You present in the Blessed Sacrament. I thank You for Your great love in giving us Your very Body and Blood, Soul and Divinity in the Eucharist. I truly believe that You are present in this great Sacrament of the Altar. Night and day, You remain with us, drawing us closer to Your Most Sacred Heart, full of compassion and mercy for us poor sinners. I offer You all my thoughts, words, deeds, and affections. Graciously accept the homage of my life. By the grace of the Holy Spirit, make me love You more and more so that I may love all others in Your Name and be pleasing to the Father. You who live and reign forever and ever. Amen.

Prayer of Petition

Father Most Merciful, I praise and thank You for the gift of Jesus, Your only begotten Son whom You sent as our Savior and Redeemer. I truly believe that Jesus who remains with us in the Most Blessed Sacrament of the Altar stands before Your throne of grace, making constant intercession for us. In His outstretched hands, I place my fervent prayer (*here mention your intentions*). Have mercy on me and answer me according to Your holy will. With full confidence in Your kindness, I offer my prayer in the Name of Jesus who lives and reigns with You in the unity of the Holy Spirit, God, forever and ever. Amen.

Prayer to Our Blessed Mother

O Mary, most blessed of all women, to you we come in humble petition. From you, Virgin Immaculate, the Son of God took flesh and became our Savior. By His Suffering, Death, and Resurrection, He has won for us the forgiveness of our sins and the gift of eternal life. Mother of the Redeemer, look with pity on us and help us grow in a greater and greater devotion to the Eucharist, the very Body and Blood, Soul

and Divinity of your beloved Son. Through your powerful intercession, Refuge of sinners, gain for us true sorrow for our sins so that we may worthily share in the Eucharist, the Sacrifice of the Cross made present to us, and, with firm faith, receive Him in Holy Communion. Mother of Divine Grace, assist us with your prayers so that our whole lives become an act of adoration and praise of Jesus who is Lord forever and ever. Amen.

O Sacrament Most Holy,
O Sacrament Divine!
All praise and all thanksgiving
be every moment Thine.

For additional prayers see page 113

Ninth Day

9

One Bread, One Body

"Whoever feeds upon my flesh and drinks my blood dwells in me and I dwell in him."
Jn 6:56

Written in bold letters across the pages of Sacred Scripture is the unmistakable fact that God calls us to cooperate with Him. On the opening pages of Genesis, God does not merely create the world and then withdraw in isolation. He settles Adam and Eve in Eden and commands them to till and tend the earth: "The Lord God took the man and placed him in the Garden of Eden so that he might work it and care for it" (Gen 2:15).

Without God the Creator, there would be no garden on earth. But, without Adam and Eve, the created vegetation would not survive or grow. From the very beginning of creation, God works with Adam and Eve and all their children.

Not only in the work of creation, but in the very mystery of our redemption has the all-perfect God chosen to work with and through imperfect individuals. With one

stroke of His outstretched arm, He could have saved Israel from slavery in Egypt. Instead, He chose to work through Moses, a flawed and less than perfect man.

This great principle of divine and human cooperation finds its highest fulfillment in the Incarnation. God became man to accomplish our redemption. He chose to work with us to bring us to the fullness of life. Throughout His public ministry, Jesus Himself, the Word made flesh, was constantly calling others to cooperate with Him.

At the marriage feast of Cana, Jesus performed His first miracle. When the wine ran out, Jesus could have supplied enough wine to continue the celebration by the power of His word alone. But He chose otherwise. He orders the servants to fill the six empty stone jars with water. Each held twenty to thirty gallons of water. He tells the steward in charge to draw some out. To the steward's amazement, it is a wine of the finest vintage. In the magnificent words of the poet Richard Crashaw, "The unconscious waters saw their God and blushed."

Jesus used the servants and the steward in charge to perform "the first of his signs at Cana in Galilee, thereby revealing his glory"

(Jn 2:11). Inviting others to work with Him, Jesus provided more than nearly one thousand bottles of the choicest wine! By all accounts, an overabundance of wine for the wedding at Cana. God is always generous in His gifts.

In the same way as at Cana, in a wilderness place near Bethsaida, Jesus works the miracle of the multiplication of the loaves and fish. He uses others to help Him. And, once again, He provides an unexpected abundance. From the preparation for the miracle to its conclusion, Jesus involves the apostles in providing the feast in the desert.

After Andrew finds five loaves and two fish, Jesus says, "Bring them to me" (Mt 14:18). It was not a request. It was a command, given with authority and assurance. Before Jesus works the miracle, He requires the obedience of His co-workers. Their very bringing of these meager supplies to Jesus is in itself an act of faith. They do not know yet what He is to do, but they trust Him. "Faith is only real when there is obedience, never without it, and faith only becomes faith in the act of obedience" (Dietrich Bonhoeffer).

When Jesus had descended the mount of Transfiguration, a man approached Him.

Jesus' disciples had been unable to cast out a demon from his son who was possessed. The distraught father brings his son to Jesus (Lk 9:37-43) and Jesus casts out the demon. No situation is impossible when we bring it to Jesus. We can always trust in His goodness to do what is best for us. He says to each of us in sufferings and trials, "Come to me all you who are weary and overburdened, and I will give you rest" (Mt 11:28).

In obedience to Jesus, the disciples bring Jesus the bread and fish and then Jesus uses them to prepare for the miracle. "He instructed his disciples, 'Make them sit down in groups…'" (Lk 9:14). With the help of the disciples, Jesus seats the crowd in rows of fifty each with one row facing the other (Mk 6:39-40). In this way, the disciples can pass between them in an orderly way to distribute the bread and fish.

Luke deliberately uses the Greek word (κατακλίνω: *kataklino*) that means not merely to sit down but to recline at a table. He is telling us that the people are arranged as guests at a banquet. It is the season of the Passover and Jesus is providing the crowd with a Passover meal in the wilderness. Like the crowds seated on the grass and not

knowing what is to happen next, we must put ourselves in ready obedience to Jesus, attentive to His command. His instructions are always the prelude to His gifts.

In the first three gospels, Jesus takes the bread, blesses it and then hands it to the disciples to distribute (Mt 14:19; Mk 6:41; Lk 9:16). When Mark and Luke tell us that Jesus "blessed" (εὐλόγησεν: *eulogēsen*) and "broke" (κατέκλασεν: *kateklasen*) the bread, they use the aorist tense of these two Greek verbs. This tense describes a single act. But when they tell us that he "gave" (ἐδίδου: *edidou*) the bread to His disciples, Mark and Luke use the imperfect tense. This indicates a continuous, repeated action. In Jesus' hands, the few loaves and fish become a banquet. The disciples take the bread and fish Jesus gives them and they distribute it to the people. When they returned to Jesus with their empty hands, His are full, ready to give them more.

At the end of the miracle, Jesus again makes use of the disciples. "When they had eaten enough, he said to the disciples, 'Gather up the fragments that are left over, so that nothing will be wasted'" (Jn 6:12). All four gospels tell us that the disciples

gathered up twelve baskets of leftovers. But only John uses the Greek word συνάγω (*sunago*) meaning "to gather." This is the very same word the Greek Old Testament uses to describe the gathering up of the manna that fell in the wilderness during the Exodus (Ex 16:16). Clearly John wants us to connect the two events, He wants us to see Jesus as providing bread from heaven for our journey to the Promised Land.

The fragments the apostles gather up are not the small crumbs that fell from the hands of the people. Rather, they are the broken pieces that came from the hands of Jesus. Jesus always provides beyond our means.

With these broken fragments, the disciples fill twelve baskets. All four gospel writers use the same word for basket (κόφινος: *kophinos*). These baskets were the small baskets Jews would carry when on a journey. In traveling among the Gentiles, Jews expected little hospitality and brought their own provisions in these baskets so as not to eat unclean food.

Most likely each of the apostles was carrying one such basket. They fill their baskets with the fragments left over. They had

helped to feed the hungry and now are richly rewarded. To give to others is to gain for oneself. When we generously share Christ's gifts with others, we ourselves come into a more ample possession of Christ Himself.

The apostles now have provisions for themselves as they journey with Jesus. Even more than that, they have provisions which they can now freely give to the poor. "The reward for work well done is the opportunity to do more" (Jonas Salk).

These full baskets also teach us that, in Christ's gift of Himself as the Bread of Life in the Eucharist, there is always more than at any given moment we can appropriate. His provision is more than enough for a hungry world. And they who share His gifts with others will always have an increase themselves. There is no surer way to receive the full blessing of Christ than to share Him with others.

Furthermore, it is by our very sharing in the Eucharist with each other that we are joined together in Christ. He dwells in us and we in Him. Thus, we truly become the Body of Christ for the world. St. Paul provided this great insight in writing to the Corinthians.

> The cup of blessing that we bless, is it not a sharing in the blood of Christ? The bread that we break, is it not a sharing in the body of Christ? Because there is one bread, we who are many are one body, for we all partake of the one bread.
>
> 1 Cor 10:16-17

Thus, when we receive the Eucharist or when we kneel in adoration before the Eucharist, we devoutly exclaim in faith, "O Sacrament of devotion! O sign of unity! O bond of charity!" (St. Augustine, *In Joannis Evangelium*, 26, 13)

> *The sacrifices of the Lord themselves highlight the unanimity of Christians strengthened by solid, indivisible charity. For when the Lord calls the bread formed of the union of many grains his body, and when he calls the wine pressed from many clusters of grapes and poured together his blood, in the same way he indicates our flock formed of a multitude united together.*
>
> St. Cyprian, Ep. *ad Magnum*, 6

PRAYERS

O God, come to my assistance.
O Lord, make haste to help me.

Glory be to the Father, and to the Son
And to the Holy Spirit.
As it was in the beginning is now
and ever shall be, world without end. Amen.

Prayer for the Ninth Day

Lord Jesus, our Eternal High Priest, on the night You were betrayed, You prayed that the Church, born from Your side on the Cross, might be always one. Grant, we pray, that we who receive the Eucharist, the sacrament of unity, may always say in word and deed "Thy will be done." Graciously pour out on us the Holy Spirit, the source of unity and the bond of charity, so that our sad divisions cease. May the Holy Spirit draw us closer to You and thus closer to each other so that, united as one body in mind, heart, and affection, we may give praise and glory to the Father together with You and the Holy Spirit, God, forever and ever. Amen.

Prayer of Adoration

Lord Jesus Christ, I adore and I worship You present in the Blessed Sacrament. I thank You for Your great love in giving us Your very Body and Blood, Soul and Divinity in the Eucharist. I truly believe that You are present in this great Sacrament of the Altar. Night and day, You remain with us, drawing us closer to Your Most Sacred Heart, full of compassion and mercy for us poor sinners. I offer You all my thoughts, words, deeds, and affections. Graciously accept the homage of my life. By the grace of the Holy Spirit, make me love You more and more so that I may love all others in Your Name and be pleasing to the Father. You who live and reign forever and ever. Amen.

Prayer of Petition

Father Most Merciful, I praise and thank You for the gift of Jesus, Your only begotten Son whom You sent as our Savior and Redeemer. I truly believe that Jesus who remains with us in the Most Blessed Sacrament of the Altar stands before Your throne of grace, making constant intercession for us. In His outstretched hands, I place my fervent prayer (*here mention your*

intentions). Have mercy on me and answer me according to Your holy will. With full confidence in Your kindness, I offer my prayer in the Name of Jesus who lives and reigns with You in the unity of the Holy Spirit, God, forever and ever. Amen.

Prayer to Our Blessed Mother

O Mary, most blessed of all women, to you we come in humble petition. From you, Virgin Immaculate, the Son of God took flesh and became our Savior. By His Suffering, Death, and Resurrection, He has won for us the forgiveness of our sins and the gift of eternal life. Mother of the Redeemer, look with pity on us and help us grow in a greater and greater devotion to the Eucharist, the very Body and Blood, Soul and Divinity of your beloved Son. Through your powerful intercession, Refuge of sinners, gain for us true sorrow for our sins so that we may worthily share in the Eucharist, the Sacrifice of the Cross made present to us, and, with firm faith, receive Him in Holy Communion. Mother of Divine Grace, assist us with your prayers so that our whole lives become an act of adoration and praise of Jesus who is Lord forever and ever. Amen.

O Sacrament Most Holy,
O Sacrament Divine!
All praise and all thanksgiving
be every moment Thine.

For additional prayers see page 113

Conclusion

The crowds that had followed Jesus into the desert near Bethsaida were anxiously awaiting the Messiah to throw off the yoke of Rome. Men such as Judas of Galilee, Theudas, Simon of Peraea, and Athronges claimed to be the Messiah. But they worked no miracles. They failed to win their freedom from Rome. And those who followed them were sorely disappointed. When Jesus multiplied the bread in the wilderness, it took very little for crowds to turn to Him to be their political savior.

The Jews expected that the Messiah would inaugurate God's kingdom by performing miracles like those of the Exodus. During the Exodus, Moses had organized people into groups of hundreds and fifties in the wilderness (Ex 18:25). The Qumran community looked forward to their Messiah to do the same. When he came, he would group his followers into hundreds and fifties and wage a victorious war against their oppressors. (*The War of the Sons of Light Against the Sons of Darkness*).

When Jesus multiplied the bread and the fish in the desert near Bethsaida, it was the

time of the Passover and Messianic expectations filled the air. As Moses had done in the wilderness, Jesus organized the crowd in groups of fifties and hundreds. And, as Moses had done, Jesus fed the crowds with bread from heaven. The miraculous feeding of the thousands immediately ignited their Messianic expectation. Jesus was the New Moses, the Prophet, the one to lead them to freedom. "When the people saw the sign he had performed, they began to say, 'This is indeed the Prophet who is to come into the world'" (Jn 6:14).

Under Moses, their ancestors had eaten the manna and the quail that came down from heaven. God gave this food not simply to satisfy their hunger, but as provisions needed for their march to freedom. Now that the multitude in the desert had eaten the bread and the fish which Jesus gave them, they were ready to carry Jesus off to Jerusalem and crown Him the king. They were ready for their march to freedom. They were eager for Him to liberate them and set up His kingdom on earth.

John graphically describes the crowd's frenzied enthusiasm when he says that they were about to carry Him off. The verb "carry

off" is the Greek word ἁρπάζειν (*arpazein*: to snatch). The word depicts the sudden swoop of the falcon seizing its prey. John wants us to realize the force they are about to use to have their way.

This is the second time Jesus is offered the crown. Before Jesus began His public ministry, Satan had been the first to offer Jesus the crown in the temptations in the desert. Jesus refused. Now during His public ministry, the people offer Him the crown. He again refuses. Only at the end of His life will He accept the crown which the Father offers Him. A crown not of gold and silver, but a crown of thorns. For by His suffering and death, He will usher in God's kingdom that outlasts every temporal power. His kingdom is not of this world (Jn 18:36).

It seems that even the disciples were caught up in the enthusiasm of the crowd. They had seen what Jesus did. They had witnessed His power. Two of the evangelists tell us that Jesus had to compel them to leave (Mt 14:22; Mk 6:45). They were hoping Jesus would set up His kingdom right then and there. They had much to learn about the type of the Messiah Jesus was. Only in the light of the Resurrection will they be able

to recognize the type of Messiah Jesus came to be.

"Jesus realized that they were going to come and carry him off (ἁρπάζειν) to make him king, so he again withdrew to the mountain by himself" (Jn 6:15). All four gospels record the fact that Jesus withdrew often to be by Himself (e.g., Mt 15:29; Mk 1:45; Lk 5:15-16; Jn 7:10). He sought the silence of solitude to find in prayer to His Father the strength He needed for His mission. But His going away by Himself had another purpose. By His separation from His disciples, He was preparing them for the day when, although He would no longer be visibly present to them, He would still be with them, assisting them with His prayer and grace.

The day after the multiplication of the loaves and fish, the crowds looked for Jesus and found Him. He spoke to them at length in the synagogue of Capernaum. In the wilderness near Bethsaida, Jesus had worked the miracle as a sign (Jn 6:14). Now He explains its true meaning.

Moses had given their ancestors manna in the desert. The bread He gave to the people the day before pointed to Jesus who is the New Manna. He is "the living bread

come down from heaven" (Jn 6:51). He is the Bread of life. He tells them, "The bread that I will give is my flesh, for the life of the world" (Jn 6:51). The multiplication of the loaves was but a foretaste of the great gift of the Eucharist.

After the Resurrection, Jesus once again provides a meal of bread and fish near the Sea of Galilee. However, He provides it only for His apostles. The apostles had returned to their former way of life as fishermen. The Risen Lord seeks them out to strengthen them for their mission. As they return to the shore after toiling all night and catching nothing, Jesus appears to them. At His word, they drop their nets and make a miraculous catch of fish.

"When they came ashore, they saw a charcoal fire with fish (ὀψάριον: *opsarion*) on it and bread" (Jn 21:9). "Jesus then… took the bread and gave it to them, and likewise the fish" (the little fish) (Jn 21:13). Even though they had dragged ashore the net full of large fish, Jesus made them bring some of the little fish (ὀψάριον: *opsarion*) they had caught. The word John uses for "little fish" is the same word he uses in the miracle of the multiplication of loaves

and fish. And he is the only evangelist to use this word.

Thus, at His last meal with His apostles, with infinite humility, Jesus feeds them exactly as He had done in the miracle of the multiplication of loaves and fish. He is reminding them and us of the great power and strength that He, our Risen Lord, will continue to give us in the Eucharist. For in this sacrament, Jesus remains with us, nourishing us with His very Body and Blood, Soul and Divinity. He stays present to us, accompanying us and drawing us into His kingdom where death has no power and we live forever.

Prayers before the Blessed Sacrament

Act of Adoration

We adore You, Most Holy Lord, Jesus Christ, here and in all the churches of the whole world, and we bless You because by Your Cross You have redeemed the world. Have mercy on us. Amen.

St. Francis of Assisi

Act of Faith

I believe in my heart and openly profess that the bread and wine which are placed upon the altar are, by the mystery of the sacred prayer and the words of the Redeemer, substantially changed into the true and life-giving Flesh and Blood of Jesus Christ Our Lord. I believe that after the Consecration there is present the true Body of Christ which was born of the Virgin Mary and offered up for the salvation of the world, hung upon the Cross, and now sits at the right hand of the Father. I believe that there is present the true Blood of Christ which flowed from His side. His Body and Blood are present not only by means of a sign and

of the efficacy of the Sacrament, but also in the very reality and truth of their nature and substance. Amen.

Pope St. Gregory VII

Prayer for Union with Christ

Lord Jesus Christ, pierce my soul with Your love so that I may always long for You alone, who are the Bread of Angels and the fulfillment of the soul's deepest desires. May my heart always hunger and feed upon You so that my soul may be filled with the sweetness of Your presence. May my soul thirst for You, who are the source of life, wisdom, knowledge, light and all the riches of God our Father. May I always seek and find You, think upon You, speak to You and do all things for the honor and glory of Your holy name. Be always my only hope, my peace, my refuge and my help in whom my heart is rooted so that I may never be separated from You. Amen.

Saint Bonaventure

Anima Christi

Soul of Christ, sanctify me.
Body of Christ, save me.
Blood of Christ, inebriate me.

Water from the side of Christ, wash me.
Passion of Christ, strengthen me.
O Good Jesus, hear me.
Within Your wounds hide me.
Permit me not to be separated from You.
From the wicked foe, defend me.
At the hour of my death, call me
and bid me come to You
That with Your saints I may praise You
For ever and ever. Amen.

Prayer for Families

O Living Bread, that came down from heaven to give life to the world! O loving shepherd of our souls, from Your throne of glory where, a "hidden God", You pour out Your grace upon families and peoples, we commend to You particularly the sick, the unhappy, the poor and all who beg for food and employment, imploring for all and every one the assistance of Your providence; we commend to You the families, so that they may be fruitful centers of Christian life. May the abundance of Your grace be poured over all. Amen.

Pope St. John XXIII

Act of Reparation

O Lord, my God and Savior,
as Thou didst endure for our salvation
the outrages of those who crucified Thee,
so now deign to bear with those
who by careless or unworthy Communions
approach and touch Thee,
not discerning Thee,
and endure all irreverences
rather than withhold Thy sacred Presence
from our Altars:
I bewail these indignities,
and most earnestly desire to prevent,
to the utmost of my power,
whatever thus still grieves Thee.
I beseech Thee,
accept this sorrow and this desire
as the only offering I can make
in reparation of so great dishonor.
O Lord, increase my faith,
and preserve me from the least profanation
of this adorable Mystery,
and kindle in me and in the hearts of all Thy people,
such reverence and devotion
that Thy most holy name may more and more be honored
and glorified in this Sacrament. Amen.

Act of Thanksgiving and Petition to God the Father with Jesus and the Blessed Virgin Mary

O most merciful Father,
who has so loved me as to give me
Thine Only-begotten Son for my food and drink,
and with Him all things,
look upon the Face of Thy Anointed,
in whom Thou art well pleased.

This Thy Beloved Son,
and with Him my heart,
I offer and present to Thee for all the blessings
Thou has this day given me.
May Thou, O Father,
be now well pleased in Him,
and through Him turn away Thy indignation from me.

Behold the One Mediator between God and men,
the Man Christ Jesus,
my Advocate and High Priest,
Who intercedes for me.
Him do I offer and plead before Thee,
who committed no sin,
but bore the sins of the world,
and by whose stripes we are healed.

Accept, therefore, O Holy Father,
this Unspotted Victim,
to the honor and glory of Thy name,
in thanksgiving for all the blessings
Thou has ever bestowed upon me,
for the remission also of my sins,
and for the supply of all my defects and shortcomings.

O Blessed Virgin,
Mother of my God and Savior,
present my petitions to thy Son.
O all you Angels and Saints, citizens of heaven,
join also your prayers with mine.
You stand always before the Throne,
and see Him face to face,
whom I here receive under veils.
Be ever mindful of me,
and obtain from Him and through Him
that with you I may bless Him
and love Him forever. Amen.

Litany of the Most Blessed Sacrament

St. Peter Julian Eymard

Lord, have mercy.
Lord, have mercy.
Christ, have mercy.
Christ, have mercy.

Lord, have mercy.
Lord, have mercy.

Christ, hear us.
Christ, graciously hear us.

God the Father of Heaven, *have mercy on us.*
God the Son, Redeemer of the world, *have mercy on us.*
God the Holy Spirit, *have mercy on us.*
Holy Trinity, one God, *have mercy on us.*

Jesus, Eternal High Priest of the Eucharistic Sacrifice, *have mercy on us.*
Jesus, Divine Victim on the Altar for our salvation, *have mercy on us.*
Jesus, hidden under the appearance of bread, *have mercy on us.*
Jesus, dwelling in the tabernacles of the world, *have mercy on us.*
Jesus, really, truly and substantially present in the Blessed Sacrament, *have mercy on us.*
Jesus, abiding in Your fullness, Body, Blood, Soul and Divinity, *have mercy on us.*
Jesus, Bread of Life, *have mercy on us.*
Jesus, Bread of Angels, *have mercy on us.*
Jesus, with us always until the end of the world, *have mercy on us.*

Sacred Host, summit and source of all worship and Christian life, *have mercy on us.*

Sacred Host, sign and cause of the unity of the Church, *have mercy on us.*

Sacred Host, adored by countless angels, *have mercy on us.*

Sacred Host, spiritual food, *have mercy on us.*

Sacred Host, Sacrament of love, *have mercy on us.*

Sacred Host, bond of charity, *have mercy on us.*

Sacred Host, greatest aid to holiness, *have mercy on us.*

Sacred Host, gift and glory of the priesthood, *have mercy on us.*

Sacred Host, in which we partake of Christ, *have mercy on us.*

Sacred Host, in which the soul is filled with grace, *have mercy on us.*

Sacred Host, in which we are given a pledge of future glory, *have mercy on us.*

Blessed be Jesus in the Most Holy Sacrament of the Altar.

Blessed be Jesus in the Most Holy Sacrament of the Altar.

Blessed be Jesus in the Most Holy Sacrament of the Altar.

For those who do not believe in Your Eucharistic presence, *have mercy, O Lord.*

For those who are indifferent to the Sacrament of Your love, *have mercy on us.*

For those who have offended You in the Holy Sacrament of the Altar, *have mercy on us.*

That we may show fitting reverence when entering Your holy temple, *we beseech You, hear us.*

That we may make suitable preparation before approaching the Altar, *we beseech You, hear us.*

That we may receive You frequently in Holy Communion with real devotion and true humility, *we beseech You, hear us.*

That we may never neglect to thank You for so wonderful a blessing, *we beseech You, hear us.*

That we may cherish time spent in silent prayer before You, *we beseech You, hear us.*

That we may grow in knowledge of this Sacrament of sacraments, *we beseech You, hear us.*

That all priests may have a profound love of the Holy Eucharist, *we beseech You, hear us.*

That they may celebrate the Holy Sacrifice of the Mass in accordance with its sublime dignity, *we beseech You, hear us.*

That we may be comforted and sanctified with Holy Viaticum at the hour of our death, *we beseech You, hear us.*

That we may see You one day face to face in Heaven, *we beseech You, hear us.*

Lamb of God, You take away the sins of the world, *spare us, O Lord.*

Lamb of God, You take away the sins of the world, *graciously hear us, O Lord.*

Lamb of God, You take away the sins of the world, *have mercy on us, O Lord.*

℣. O Sacrament Most Holy, O Sacrament Divine,

℟. All praise and all thanksgiving be every moment Thine.

Let us pray,

Most merciful Father,
You continue to draw us to Yourself

through the Eucharistic Mystery.
Grant us fervent faith in this Sacrament of love,
in which Christ the Lord Himself is contained, offered and received.
Through the same Christ our Lord. Amen.

Divine Praises

Blessed be God.
Blessed be His Holy Name.
Blessed be Jesus Christ, true God and true Man.
Blessed be the Name of Jesus.
Blessed be His Most Sacred Heart.
Blessed be His Most Precious Blood.
Blessed be Jesus in the Most Holy Sacrament of the Altar.
Blessed be the Holy Spirit, the Paraclete.
Blessed be the great Mother of God, Mary most Holy.
Blessed be her Holy and Immaculate Conception.
Blessed be her Glorious Assumption.
Blessed be the name of Mary, Virgin and Mother.
Blessed be St. Joseph, her most chaste spouse.
Blessed be God in His Angels and in His Saints. Amen.

Bishop Emeritus Arthur J. Serratelli was the seventh bishop of the Diocese of Paterson, N.J. He is present chairman for the Vatican's Dialogue between the Catholic Church and the World Alliance of Baptists. He has served as chairman of the International Commission on English in the Liturgy; member of the Vatican's Congregation of Divine Worship and the Discipline of the Sacraments; and member of Vox Clara. He has served a three-year term as chairman of the Committee for the Translation of Sacred Scripture of the United States Conference of Catholic Bishops; twice chairman of the Committee on Divine Worship of the United States Conference of Catholic Bishops; chairman of the Committee on Doctrine; and member of the Subcommittee for the Review of Catechetical Texts. As a Professor of Sacred Scripture and Systematics, he has taught in three major seminaries. He continues to give retreats, lectures, and courses in Sacred Scripture as well as doing pastoral work in a parish.

This is the Bishop's seventh book. His previous books are: *From the Cross to the Empty Tomb*, *The Seven Gifts of the Holy Spirit*, *Jesus' Last Days*, *The Scriptural Novena to St. Joseph*, *The Parables of Jesus* and *Eucharistic Adoration.*

JESUS' LAST DAYS

Most Rev. Arthur J. Serratelli, S.T.D., S.S.L., D.D.

Through Bishop Serratelli's reflections on the similar accounts of the four evangelists, we relive Jesus' Passion bathed in the light of Easter glory. We will appreciate how the Cross remains the instrument of our salvation and see more clearly our own call to discipleship. 128 pages. Size 5 x 7.

No. 932/04—Flexible cover **6.95**
ISBN 978-1-9-47070-35-6

THE SEVEN GIFTS OF THE HOLY SPIRIT

Most Rev. Arthur J. Serratelli, S.T.D., S.S.L., D.D.

Through history, art, Scripture, and Catholic documents, you will appreciate and grasp more fully how the seven gifts of the Holy Spirit can help you to live a truly authentic Christian life filled with peace and joy. 96 pages. Size 4 3/8 x 6 3/4.

No. 930/04—Flexible cover............. **5.95**
ISBN 978-1-947070-23-3

catholicbookpublishing.com

FROM THE CROSS TO THE EMPTY TOMB

Most Rev. Arthur J. Serratelli, S.T.D., S.S.L., D.D.

The author invites you to journey with those who were with Jesus in His last hours. You may be like Peter one day, and like Judas, Simon, Mary Magdalene, or Our Lady on another. This Lenten book provides a deeper appreciation for God's eternal saving love.

96 pages. Size 4 3/8 x 6 3/4.

No. 928/04—Flexible cover **6.95**

ISBN 978-1-947070-13-4

THE PARABLES OF JESUS

Most Rev. Arthur J. Serratelli, S.T.D., S.S.L., D.D.

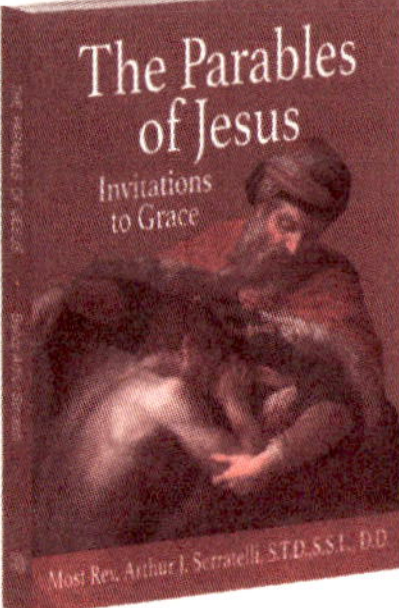

Follow Jesus through His interaction with farmers, shepherds, aristocrats, religious and political leaders, and laborers in 13 parables filled with contrast, exaggeration, humor, and surprise that represent more than one third of His teachings. Both the scholar and student, the expert and the layperson can draw inspiration from the greatest storyteller the world has ever known. Even lifetime Catholics who think they know the parables will be rewarded with the wisdom and history that the author shares on these beloved, grace-filled stories.

176 pages. Size 5 1/4 x 7 3/4.

No. 934/04—Flexible cover... **7.95**

ISBN 978-1-953152-08-4

catholicbookpublishing.com

SCRIPTURAL NOVENA TO SAINT JOSEPH

Most Rev. Arthur J. Serratelli, S.T.D., S.S.L., D.D.

Written with deep devotion and respect for Jesus' earthly father, these nine biblical reflections will help you to grow in your knowledge and love of the Church's holy patron, St. Joseph.

You, your family, and the Church will be blessed by praying to the holy, humble, just, and trustworthy St. Joseph. He has the power to assist and protect us as he did most perfectly for Mary and their Son. 96 pages. Size 4 3/8 x 6 3/4.

No. 946/04—Paperback cover.. **5.95**
ISBN 978-1-953152-30-5

EUCHARISTIC ADORATION Scriptural Reflections And Prayers

Most Rev. Arthur J. Serratelli, S.T.D., S.S.L., D.D.

The Bishop's deep spirituality, faith, knowledge, and love of the Eucharist will often leave you breathless. Meditate before, after, and during Adoration with a fervent desire to become a living host of Jesus, the perfect Host for all. 176 pages. Size 4 3/8 x 6 3/4.

No. 947/19—Dura-Lux cover **11.95**
ISBN 978-1-953152-60-2

catholicbookpublishing.com

St. Joseph BIBLE HANDBOOK — In addition to a general introduction to each book of the Bible, the main headings found in every book—the *Outline, Frequently Asked Questions, Study Questions,* and *Look out for...*— succinctly point to the valuable information contained in the pages of the Bible. 256 pages. Size 6 3/4 x 9 1/2.

No. 649/04—Durable cover **19.95**

ISBN 978-1-941243-98-5

St. Joseph NEW CATHOLIC BIBLE NEW TESTAMENT — This readable study edition has a large, easy-to-read typeface, complete notes and references, self-explaining maps, a handy Study Guide, a Bible Dictionary, the words of Christ in red, photographs, and many other features. Ideal for schools and Bible study. 528 pages. Size 6 1/2 x 9 1/4.

No. 311/19—Burgundy Dura-Lux cover....... **17.95**

ISBN: 978-1-947070-66-0

DAY BY DAY WITH St. Joseph — By Msgr. Joseph Champlin and Msgr. Ken Lasch. Pray with St. Joseph every day of the year with a Scripture verse, short reflection, and prayer focusing on his deep faith, trust, and love for God, his family, and the Church. 192 pages. Size 4 x 6 1/4.

No. 162/19—Dura-Lux cover **9.95**

ISBN 978-1-937913-08-3

St. Joseph: MAN OF FAITH — By Jacques Gauthier. This book focuses on the excerpts of the New Testament in which St. Joseph appears, speaks of his veneration, and concludes with some prayers that will awaken our contemplative glance on this Patron of the Church and of workers. Illustrated. 96 pages. Size 4 1/4 x 6 3/4.

No. 72/04—Flexible cover............................... **4.95**

ISBN 978-1-937913-94-6

catholicbookpublishing.com

ISBN 978-1-953152-82-4
90000
9 781953 152824